THE HAPPY HUSBAND COOKBOOK

First Edition, 2011

Nashville Kat

Tin Boot Publishing
Underwood, IA. 51576

Tin Boot Publishing
P.O. Box 112
Underwood, IA. 51576
E-mail: happycanteen@yahoo.com

ISBN 978-0-9834882-0-0

Printed in the United States of America

TABLE OF CONTENTS

FORWARD

When I got married, I was thrilled that I now had someone to cook for every night of the week, so my husband is the true inspiration behind this book. These 204 recipes are my absolute best; all regularly used; tried and true. It is such a blessing to be able to share them with you!

Growing up, my mom was an amazing cook but with six in our family, she often tried to stretch the budget. She would put powdered milk in the regular milk carton or she would pass beef heart off as a roast, but my brother Mark and sisters Lynn and Amy and I figured it out every time. We loved it when my parents went out to eat because then we got to pick out a TV dinner and I always chose Swanson's fried chicken with whipped potatoes, mixed vegetables and apple cobbler; it was the perfect meal! My brother also had a game we played when our parents were gone. He'd sit by the kitchen light switch and every time he turned the lights off, my sisters and I had to freeze. He always looked for us to be in mid-bite so he could freeze us for as long as he wanted. All we could do was moan for him to turn the lights back on, all without moving our lips because after all; we were frozen.

It is my prayer that *THE HAPPY HUSBAND COOKBOOK* will get you eating as a family, that it will inspire you to have dinner parties, and that it will teach you that cooking builds bridges to people. When I have friends over for dinner, I usually make one new thing so we can test it together. I encourage you to try that too. You just might surprise yourself with a new treasure for your recipe collection. My great hope is that the pages of this book will be stained in many places because it is *used*!

You can reach me at happycanteen@yahoo.com, or www.nashvillekat.com

God bless you,
Kat

Jesus said, *"Man shall not live by bread alone,*
but by every word that comes from the mouth of God."

ACKNOWLEDGEMENTS

Thank you to…
Jesus Christ, for loving me unconditionally and for setting me free!

My husband, for always trying everything I've ever made in the kitchen. You're my inspiration everyday and I love you so much! My husband goes by 'Canteen Slim' and his artwork is my cover plus he did the drawings inside.

My mom, for always being there to answer all my "how do you do this" recipe questions. My mom is really smart and she just knows stuff.

My dad, for teaching me that the way that I talk to people is so important.

Kathy Westendorp, for her computer skills and for teaching me, "Blessed are the flexible for they shall not be bent out of shape!"

Maverick Engelhart at maverickdesigngroup.com, for designing the front and back cover plus styling my photo.

Jenna Stulgies, for the back cover photography.

THINGS TO KEEP IN MIND...

*All ovens are not the same so when making a recipe for the first time, *watch it closely,* it may need more or less cooking time than specified.
*I rarely cook with garlic, so please add it as you see fit.
*My recipes always call for salted butter unless I specify to use unsalted.
*Where I use milk in any recipe, savory or sweet, any and all types will work.
*Where I use flour, I've learned any kind works.
*I use unflavored coconut oil for frying—the only oil that does not turn unhealthy when heated. I love it mixed with melted butter on popcorn.
* My go-to cooking temperature for most single item savory things is 400° for 20 minutes – burgers, pork cutlets, fish fillets, meatballs, etc. They are always cooked to perfection every time!

U.S. DRY VOLUME MEASUREMENTS:

1/16 teaspoon = dash

1/8 teaspoon = a pinch

3 teaspoons = 1 tablespoon

1/8 cup = 2 tablespoons

1/4 cup = 4 tablespoons

⅓ cup = 5 tablespoons plus 1 teaspoon

½ cup = 8 tablespoons

¾ cup = 12 tablespoons

1 cup = 16 tablespoons

1 pound = 16 ounces

U.S. TO METRIC CONVERSIONS:

1 teaspoon = 5 ml

1 tablespoon = 15 ml

1 fluid ounce = 30 ml

1 cup = 240 ml

2 cups (1 pint) = 470 ml

4 cups (1 quart) = .95 liter

1 ounce = 28 grams

1 pound = 454 grams

U.S. TO METRIC BAKING PAN CONVERSIONS:

9 X 13-inch baking dish = 22 X 33-centimeter baking dish

8 X 8-inch baking dish = 20 X 20-centimeter baking dish

9 X 5-inch loaf pan = 23 X 12-centimeter baking dish

9-inch cake pan = 22-centimeter baking dish

FAHRENHEIT TO CELSIUS:

$275° = 140° C$

$300° = 150° C$

$325° = 165° C$

$350° = 180° C$

$375° = 190° C$

$400° = 200° C$

$425° = 220° C$

$450° = 230° C$

1

BREAKFAST

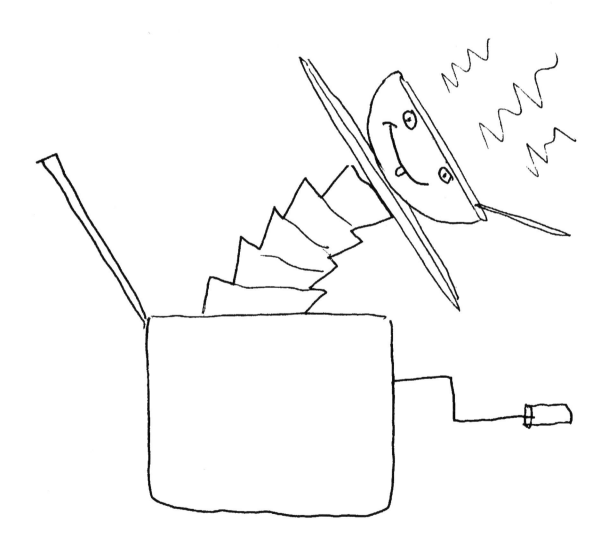

Breakfast Casserole

This is even good without the sausage. You can make this a day ahead. Put it in the refrigerator overnight to be baked the next day. The crescent dough also spreads out easier if it is at room temperature.

2 cans crescent rolls (can also use the crescent roll full sized sheets)
7 eggs
1 pound sausage, cooked and drained
1 ½ pounds sharp Cheddar cheese, shredded
¾ cup milk
1 small onion, finely diced
Big pinch of salt
Black pepper to taste

Preheat oven to 350°. Unroll one can of crescent rolls. Leave it in one long strip, pressing the perforations together. Press this on the bottom of a 9x13-inch pan which has been sprayed with cooking spray. Bake 6 minutes then take out of the oven and set aside. While that bakes, beat eggs, add milk then add salt and pepper. Sprinkle the sausage evenly on top of the crescent roll bottom then add the onion evenly then the cheese. Pour the eggs over all. Unroll the other can of crescent rolls, pushing perforations together and leaving it as one strip roll it to a 9x13-inch size and place it on top of the entire casserole. Brush the crescent roll top with beaten egg white and bake for 40 minutes.

Fern's Flap-Jacks

My Aunt Phyllis's mother-in-law Fern gave her this recipe over 50 years ago and now they're the only pancakes we'll eat. I make extra and freeze them separately to pop in the toaster for a quick meal.

3 eggs
1 ½ cups buttermilk
1 tablespoon baking powder
½ teaspoon baking soda
1 tablespoon white sugar
1 cup flour

Beat the eggs, then add everything else. Ladle batter on a hot griddle and flip them once bubbles form all over the pancake.

Dutch Pancake

This is a classic Dutch treat that I had at a friend's in Minnesota. It tastes a lot like French toast but it is easier and great for big gatherings! The finished dish is abstract peaks and valleys and it never ends up the same way twice. Very good reheated too!

4 eggs
1 ½ cups flour
1 ½ cups milk
¼ teaspoon salt
¼ cup butter
1 tablespoon lemon juice

Put the butter in a 9x13-inch pan and put that in your oven and turn it to 400°. Mix eggs, flour, lemon juice, milk and salt together and pour into your prepared pan that has the melted butter and bake 30 minutes. This is delicious with butter and maple syrup but here are some other variations. Before baking you could add: 1) Sliced apples tossed in cinnamon and brown sugar. 2) Canned pie filling. 3) Ham or bacon and shredded cheese.
4) Orange zest, cream cheese cut into cubes and powdered sugar.

Mouth Meltin' Muffins

People who don't like dates won't even taste them. This is the best muffin I've ever had.

1 cup rolled oats (quick or old-fashioned)
1 cup buttermilk
½ cup brown sugar, firmly packed
½ cup oil
2 large egg whites
1 cup flour
2 teaspoons baking powder
½ teaspoon baking soda
¾ cup dates, chopped
¾ cup pecans, chopped

In bowl combine oats, buttermilk, sugar, oil and egg whites. In another bowl combine flour, baking powder, baking soda, dates and nuts. Add both mixtures together and stir until just moistened. Pour batter into 12 paper-lined muffin tins, all the way to the top. Bake at 375° for 25 minutes.

Grandma Bert's Cinnamon Rolls

One of the many wonderful things my grandma made that remains a classic today.

2 loaves of frozen bread dough, thawed
1 cup brown sugar, firmly packed
½ cup butter, melted
¼ cup water
1 tablespoon plus 1 teaspoon cinnamon
1 cup pecans, chopped
Frosting is optional and recipe follows

Mix together brown sugar, butter, water and cinnamon. Pour that into 9x13-inch pan. Sprinkle nuts evenly the sugar mixture. Snip the loaves of dough with scissors over the pan to cover the entire surface. Let rise for two hours then bake at 350° for 30-35 minutes. Can also make this ahead and refrigerate it over night. If you do that, take it out the next day and let it sit out for 30 minutes before baking. When it is done baking, flip the whole pan over onto a platter so the syrup runs into the bread. You can then add frosting, but they are excellent without the frosting too.

Frosting (optional):
4 ounces cream cheese, softened
¼ cup butter, softened
1 cup powdered sugar
½ teaspoon vanilla
1 ½ teaspoons milk

Beat all together and spread on the warm cinnamon rolls.

Food Fact:

An etiquette writer of the 1840's advised, "Ladies may wipe their lips on the tablecloth, but not blow their noses on it."

Sour Cream Scones

I had these at a tea we had at church. They're the perfect scone!

2 cups flour
⅓ cup white sugar
1 teaspoon baking powder
¼ teaspoon baking soda
½ teaspoon salt
½ cup butter, frozen
½ cup sour cream
1 egg
½ cup additive of your choice (raisins, fresh fruit, chocolate chips etc.)
White sugar to sprinkle on top

Preheat oven to 400°. Mix flour, sugar, baking powder, baking soda and salt. Grate butter into flour and work together with hands so it resembles a course meal. Stir in your additive. In another bowl whisk sour cream and egg then using a fork, combine this with your dry ingredients until it just starts to come together. Knead dough until it starts to come together (it will be dry). Place dough on lightly floured surface. If you keep the dough in one ball you will get 8 larger scones. If you separate it in two balls you'll get 16 smaller scones. Flatten the dough in a circle that is one inch thick. Cut it into eights (or 16th's) leaving all the scones connected. Sprinkle sugar on top and place on a parchment paper lined pan and bake for 15-17 minutes.

Slap Dash Hash

True comfort food and it has just the right tang thanks to the sour cream. It is even good cold and it freezes well too.

30 ounce bag frozen hash browns
8 ounces cooked ground beef or sausage (optional)
1 - 10 ¾ ounce can cream of mushroom soup
1 - 10 ¾ ounce can cream of potato soup
16 ounces sour cream
½ cup butter, melted
1 medium onion, chopped
6 cups shredded Cheddar cheese (I do three cups of extra sharp white Cheddar and three cups extra sharp yellow Cheddar)
Black pepper to taste
3 cups crushed corn flakes

Preheat oven to 375°. Mix hash browns, meat (if using), soups, sour cream, butter, onion, two cups cheddar and pepper to taste. With your hands, pack into a 9x13-inch pan; sprinkle with remaining cheese and corn flakes and bake one hour. If you made this ahead and it came out of the refrigerator cold, bake it one hour, 20 minutes. Half way thru you may have to cover it with foil so the corn flakes don't burn.

```
                        Food Fact:
During the Alaskan Klondike gold rush of 1897, potatoes were
  so valued for their vitamin C that miners traded gold for
                         potatoes.
```

Egg-Zactly Cheesy Casserole

I have been making this for years and it goes fast because it is so good!

1 pound pepper jack cheese, shredded
1 pound Monterey Jack cheese, shredded
10 eggs
⅔ cup flour
3 ⅓ cups half-and-half
8 ounces diced green chilies, drained
½ cup salsa

Preheat oven to 375°. Mix cheeses together and spread evenly in buttered 9X13-inch pan. Beat eggs, whisk in flour slowly, and then whisk in half-and-half. Pour egg mixture over cheeses in pan. Place chilies evenly on top of that then spoon the salsa evenly over. Bake for 45 minutes or until the center is set.

Creamy Hot Chocolate Mix

The best hot chocolate with deep, deep chocolate flavor. You will want this often!

7 cups powdered milk
2 - 5 ounce packages cook and serve chocolate pudding mix
3 cups powdered chocolate drink mix
½ cup powdered non dairy creamer
¾ cup powdered sugar
1 cup unsweetened cocoa powder

Mix together and store in airtight container. A serving is ⅓ cup of the mix to one cup of boiling water.

Farm Hand Omelet

Perfect omelet for 2 hungry people. We have it for dinner often.

4 - sausage patties
2 - 3 ounce extra sharp Cheddar cheese, small dice, plus extra for garnish
1 tablespoon butter
1 cup potatoes, cut into small cubes
½ cup onion, chopped
2 tablespoons jalapeno peppers, minced
6 eggs
2 tablespoons milk
½ teaspoon salt
½ teaspoon black pepper

Preheat oven to 350°. Cook sausage in medium pan and set aside. In another pan, add butter, potato and onion and cook on medium for 10 minutes, stirring occasionally. Add jalapeno, cook 30 seconds and turn heat off. Beat eggs, milk, salt and pepper with a fork then add cheese. Add egg mixture to potato mixture and bake for 20 minutes or until the eggs are almost cooked in the center. Sprinkle with a handful of shredded cheese and continue baking until the cheese melts.

Nuts and Twigs Granola

I lowered the calories by swapping half the oil for applesauce and you'd never know. This is incredible granola!

8 cups rolled oats (quick or old-fashioned)
2 cups oat bran (process oats in a blender to a coarse powder)
1 cup almonds, chopped
1 cup pecans, chopped
1 cup walnuts, chopped
1 cup sunflower seeds
¼ cup brown sugar, firmly packed
¼ cup maple syrup
¼ cup honey (plus more to drizzle at the end of baking)
½ cup olive oil (light, regular or extra-virgin all work)
½ cup applesauce
1 tablespoon vanilla extract
2 ½ cups raisins or dried cranberries

Preheat oven to 325°. Line two large baking sheets with foil. Combine oats, oat bran and seeds and nuts. In a pan combine sugar, syrup, honey, oil, applesauce and vanilla. Bring to a boil over medium, then pour over the oat mixture and stir to coat. Spread evenly on baking sheets and bake 12 minutes. Then stir it and bake 30 minutes longer. Stir it again and bake 20 minutes more. Drizzle as much additional honey as you want over the oat mixture and toss to combine. Lower the oven temperature to 225° and bake 15 minutes more. Stir in the cranberries or raisins when it is completely cool.

```
                          Food Fact:
   Honey has antibacterial properties which combat infections
    and speeds the healing process. Wounds treated with honey
              heal faster and there's less scarring.
```

2

APPETIZERS AND DIPS

Home Run Cheese Ball

This makes 4 softball size balls and it is great cold on crackers but I think it is even better spread on sourdough bread and baked in the oven until warm and gooey.

2 - 8 ounce packages cream cheese, softened
10 ounces Cheddar cheese, shredded
8 ounces Gorgonzola or blue cheese, softened
½ small onion, diced
1 ½ tablespoons Worcestershire sauce
½ teaspoon cayenne pepper
3 cups toasted pecans, finely chopped
½ cup parsley, chopped

In food processor add everything except parsley and pecans. You can process this by hand too using a mixer. After mixture is processed, stir in the parsley and one cup of nuts. Put mixture in refrigerator for an hour then remove and shape into four balls. Roll in remaining nuts. Wrap each ball separately in plastic wrap and store in freezer if you aren't going to use it right away.

Jalapeno Popper Dip

This is really creamy and the flavors just burst in your mouth! Kids love it too!

4 - 8 ounce packages cream cheese, softened
2 cups mayonnaise
2 - 4 ounce cans green chilies, drained and chopped
4 ounces pickled jalapeno peppers, drained and diced
2 cups Parmesan cheese, shredded
½ cup bread crumbs

Preheat oven to 375°. Mix together the Parmesan and bread crumbs then set aside. Beat the cream cheese and mayonnaise together until smooth. Stir in chilies and jalapeno peppers and pour into a 9x13-inch pan. Sprinkle with Parmesan cheese mixture and bake for 35 minutes.

Lemon Tahini Dip

Incredible over steamed vegetables and rice. Makes a great salad dressing as well.

⅛ medium onion, cut in large pieces
1 celery stalk
¾ cup olive oil (light, regular or extra-virgin all work)
2 tablespoons water
2 tablespoons soy sauce
⅓ cup lemon juice
¾ cup prepared tahini sauce
½ tablespoon honey

Add all to a blender and process until well blended. Store in the refrigerator.

Tangy Mustard Dip

We always seem to have this in our fridge. The Dijon makes it nice and tangy.

4 heaping tablespoons raw almonds
5 tablespoons nutritional yeast flakes (purchased at health food store)
2 tablespoons soy sauce
3 tablespoons lemon juice
1 ½ tablespoons Dijon mustard
1 cup olive oil (light, regular or extra-virgin all work)
1 cup water

Combine all of this in a blender and blend until it is thick and creamy. Store in refrigerator. Use as a dip for carrots, celery or crackers. Can be used as a salad dressing.

Wipe Your Chin Dip

Creamy with just the right blend of flavors – use it as a dip with my Buffalo Wing Dings but it is also great on a salad, baked potatoes, taco chips or crackers!

16 ounces sour cream
1 ounce package dry ranch dressing mix
8 ounces blue cheese or Gorgonzola crumbles
2 tablespoons chives, chopped

Whisk all together until well mixed. Store in the refrigerator.

Pickled Beet Eggs

A treat that I can't stop eating, they are like candy to me. If you like pickled beets you will love these!

Juice drained from a can of beets (not pickled beets)
¾ cup white vinegar
¼ cup brown sugar, firmly packed
½ teaspoon salt
12 whole cloves
6 hard-boiled eggs

Put eggs in a large pot and add water to cover the eggs. Once the pot comes to a boil, cover the pan and turn the heat off. After 20 minutes, take pot off burner then pour cold water on the eggs, and remove them from the pan to cool. Mix beet juice, vinegar, sugar, salt and cloves in a pan. Bring to a boil then remove from heat and cool. Place eggs in a quart jar. Add juice mixture. To keep eggs immersed, fill a small plastic zip bag with water, fasten securely and place it on top of eggs. Refrigerate 2-3 days before eating; the longer they sit the better.

Salty Sweet Olive Tapenade

The maple syrup cuts the saltiness perfectly. It is good on crackers; amazing on fish; great on salads! These amounts are very forgiving, you can't make it wrong.

32 ounces green olives, drained and chopped
13 ounces Kalamata olives, drained and chopped
7 ounces capers, drained and chopped
8.5 ounces sun-dried tomatoes in oil, chopped
6 ounces maple syrup
Olive oil to taste (light, regular or extra-virgin all work)

Mix all together and store in the refrigerator. I think it is best served at room temperature though.

Stuffed Eggs

This is inspired by Loretta, my former neighbor.

12 large eggs
4 tablespoons mayonnaise
2 teaspoons white sugar
2 teaspoons white vinegar
2 teaspoons prepared mustard
½ teaspoon salt
Paprika for garnish

Put eggs in a large pot and add water to cover. Bring to a boil then cover the pan and turn the heat off. After 20 minutes, take pot off burner then pour cold water on the eggs then remove them from the pan to cool. When the eggs are cool, cut them in half lengthwise. Carefully remove the yolks and put them in a bowl. Mash them with a fork till they are still a bit chunky then add sugar, mayonnaise, vinegar, mustard and salt. Put the egg yolk mixture back into your halved egg whites and sprinkle liberally with paprika.

3

SALADS AND DRESSINGS

Ramen Crunch Salad

Every time I serve this, everyone always wants the recipe!

1 cup white sugar
1 cup olive oil (light, regular or extra-virgin all work)
½ cup apple cider vinegar
1 tablespoon plus 1 teaspoon soy sauce
¼ teaspoon black pepper
Red pepper flakes to taste
1 ½ packages dry ramen noodles, broken up into small pieces
2 tablespoons butter
1 ½ cups broccoli, chopped small
1 small head Romaine lettuce, cut into bite-size pieces
3 green onions, sliced
½ cup chopped walnuts (toasting is not necessary)

Sauté the dry ramen noodles in butter until golden. Set aside. Blend together: sugar, oil, vinegar, soy sauce, pepper and red pepper flakes. Set aside. In a large bowl, combine broccoli, lettuce, green onions and walnuts. Right before serving, toss in ramen noodles and dressing.

Honey Lime Watermelon

Easy and very refreshing! If you picked a melon that isn't that sweet, this will make it great! To choose the best melon, pick on that has a lot of yellow on it and sounds hollow when you knock on it.

Slices of watermelon, as much as you want
Lime zest, as much as you want
Honey to taste

Lay watermelon slices on a large platter. Drizzle watermelon liberally with honey, then sprinkle lime zest evenly over that.

Mrs. Waddlesnort's Spinach Salad

Buttery and delicious! Even if you don't like spinach, try this.

1 tablespoon butter
¾ cup slivered almonds
1 bag pre-washed spinach
1 cup dried cranberries
2 tablespoons sesame seeds, toasted
1 tablespoon poppy seeds
½ cup white sugar
2 teaspoons onion, minced
¼ teaspoon paprika
¼ cup white wine vinegar
¼ cup apple cider vinegar
½ cup olive or vegetable oil

Add butter and almonds to pan, stir as they become golden then cool. In a bowl, add spinach, almonds, sesame seeds and cranberries. Whisk together sugar, onion, both vinegars, paprika, poppy seeds and oil. Toss with spinach mixture just before serving. *You can also add crisp bacon, blue cheese, feta or gorgonzola.

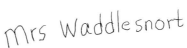

Mrs Waddlesnort

Mushroom Parmesan Salad

I never liked raw mushrooms until I made this. It is light and the more Parmesan you add, the better!

1 pound button or crimini mushrooms, thinly sliced
⅓ cup parsley, chopped
¼ cup olive oil (light, regular or extra-virgin all work)
¼ cup lemon juice
¼ teaspoon salt
½ teaspoon black pepper
Chunk of Parmesan cheese, as much as you want

Combine mushrooms and parsley then add oil, lemon juice, salt and black pepper. With a vegetable peeler, shave on large strips of Parmesan and serve.

Best Bread Salad

I have eaten many bread salads but this one beats them all! It's good the next day too.

1 cup olive oil (light, regular or extra-virgin all work)
¼ cup balsamic vinegar
1 tablespoon white sugar
1 tablespoon dried oregano
1 teaspoon black pepper
1 teaspoon salt
½ cup sun-dried tomatoes in oil, cut into thin strips
1 loaf day old sourdough, cut into bite sized chunks
1 bunch basil, cut into thin strips
1 cup Kalamata olives, rough chopped
1 cup Roma tomatoes, rough chopped

Combine olive oil, vinegar, sugar, oregano, pepper and salt then set aside. In bowl, combine sun-dried tomatoes, sourdough, basil, olives and tomatoes. Add dressing and let sit for at least 30 minutes at room temperature before serving.

Prospectors Salad

My aunt Mary Lou's masterpiece that you will serve it often! Must be stored in the refrigerator. I think it is best at room temperature.

Fresh baby spinach, as much as you want

Apples, unpeeled, cored and diced, as much as you want

Salted peanuts, as much as you want

2 large eggs

1 cup heavy cream, divided

⅓ cup apple cider vinegar

½ cup white sugar

2 tablespoons dry mustard

½ teaspoon salt

Black pepper to taste

Beat eggs and pour in small saucepan. Whisk in sugar, mustard, pepper and salt. Add a half cup of heavy cream and vinegar. Cook on low heat until thickened, stirring occasionally. When it is the thickness you like, remove from the heat and whisk in the rest of the cream. Let it set until it reaches room temperature then toss with spinach, apples and peanuts and serve immediately. It also makes a great mustard if you don't add the extra cream.

Avocado, Gorgonzola, Pear Salad

The combination of avocado, pear and gorgonzola just makes your mouth dance.

1 large head of Romaine lettuce, cut into bite-size pieces
3 pears, chopped (can also substitute chopped apple or mandarin oranges)
5 ounces Gorgonzola cheese, crumbled (can also use feta)
1 avocado, diced
½ cup green onions, sliced
¼ cup plus 1 ½ teaspoons white sugar
½ cup pecans
⅓ cup olive oil (light, regular or extra-virgin all work)
3 tablespoons red wine vinegar
1 ½ teaspoons prepared mustard
½ teaspoon salt
Black pepper to taste

In a skillet over medium heat, stir ¼ cup of sugar together with the pecans. Continue stirring gently until sugar has melted and has coated the pecans. Transfer nuts onto waxed paper. Allow them to cool then break into pieces. For the dressing; blend oil, vinegar, 1 ½ teaspoons sugar, mustard, salt and pepper. In a large serving bowl, add lettuce, pears, Gorgonzola, avocado and green onions. Right before serving, pour dressing over salad, sprinkle with pecans and serve.

```
                         Food fact:
   Cast iron skillets used to be the leading source of iron in
                      the American diet.
```

Cabin Caviar

Make it a day ahead for an even better taste. Serve with corn chips.

2 - 11 ounce cans black-eyed peas
2 - 11 ounce cans corn
6 Roma tomatoes, chopped
1 red pepper, chopped
5 green onions, sliced
1 bottle prepared Italian salad dressing
2 tablespoons lime juice
Handful of cilantro, chopped
4 ounces feta cheese, crumbled
1 - 4 ½ ounce can sliced black olives, drained and rinsed

Mix all ingredients, refrigerate at least two hours then add cilantro and feta.

Parmesan Garlic Dressing

Really, really, really good. It can also be stored at room temperature.

1 cup olive oil (light, regular or extra-virgin all work)
4 tablespoons onions, grated then chopped
2 teaspoons garlic, chopped
2 tablespoons Parmesan cheese
1 ½ teaspoons Worcestershire sauce
1 ½ teaspoons dry mustard
1 ½ teaspoons oregano
1 ½ teaspoons basil
1 ½ teaspoons white sugar
1 ½ teaspoons black pepper
½ cup red wine vinegar
2 tablespoons lemon juice
Salt to taste

Whisk all ingredients and serve it on salad or use as a dip for warm bread.

Caramelized Almond Orange Salad

Just the right mix of oranges, onions, red pepper flakes and candied almonds.

1 - 15 ounce mandarin oranges, drained
1 small red onion, sliced thin
2 heads romaine lettuce, chopped
⅔ cup sugar
1 cup almonds, sliced

To caramelize almonds:
Stir ⅔ cup sugar over medium heat until dissolved. Add almonds and stir until they are well coated. Cook until they are toasted then put on wax paper to cool. When cooled, break up into pieces as best you can.

Dressing:
⅔ cup olive oil (light, regular or extra-virgin all work)
⅓ cup vinegar
⅓ cup white sugar
1 tablespoon dried parsley
1 teaspoon salt
¼ teaspoon black pepper
¼ teaspoon red pepper flakes

Toss together the lettuce, oranges, onion, almonds and the dressing and serve immediately.

Lemon Maple Fruit Salad

I made this up years ago and it's a hit every time. You can use whatever fruit you want, just make sure it is all cut in the same sized pieces. I make this about an hour before serving so the flavors can meld together.

Gently mix together as much as you want of the following:
Apple chunks, kiwi chunks, fresh blackberries, fresh raspberries, freshly chopped mint, maple syrup, lemon juice and lemon zest.

The Best Layered Salad

Another amazing thing my mom made for us growing up.

1 head of iceberg lettuce, chopped
¼ cup onion, sliced thin
2 cups celery, chopped
1 large or smaller can sliced water chestnuts, rinsed and drained
1 - 10 ounce package frozen peas
1 ½ cups Cheddar cheese, shredded
10 slices bacon, cooked crispy (optional)
3 cups mayonnaise
3 tablespoons white sugar
Salt and pepper to taste

Mix mayonnaise and sugar in bowl and set aside. Layer salad in this order; ½ the lettuce, ½ the onion, ½ the celery, ½ the water chestnuts, ½ the peas, ½ the cheese and ½ the bacon. On top of that add ½ the mayonnaise/sugar mixture. Repeat vegetable layers, add the rest of the mayonnaise/sugar mix and top with cheese and bacon. Place it in the refrigerator at least two hours.

Classic Mustard Dressing

I often double this recipe as it is great to always have on hand. I also store it at room temperature.

½ cup olive oil (light, regular or extra-virgin all work)
1 tablespoon Dijon mustard, or any kind of spicy brown mustard you like
4 tablespoons red wine vinegar
2 teaspoons honey
¼ teaspoon salt
½ teaspoon black pepper
1 tablespoon dried parsley

Whisk mustard, vinegar, sugar, salt, pepper and parsley. Then add oil and mix.

Tangy Tater Toss

I tweaked and tweaked to get the perfect potato salad and this it is!

5 cups red or Yukon Gold potatoes, cut in bite size cubes with skins on
6 hard-boiled eggs
2 stalks of celery, chopped
½ cup sweet relish
½ cup green onions, sliced
⅓ cup lemon juice
3 tablespoons white sugar
1 ½ teaspoons Worcestershire sauce
1 teaspoon dry mustard
2 tablespoons prepared mustard
1 cup mayonnaise
1 tablespoon apple cider vinegar
1 teaspoon salt
¼ teaspoon black pepper

Boil potatoes for 15 minutes then drain and blot dry. Combine the potatoes with everything else, mix well and put in the refrigerator for at least two hours. *To hard-boil eggs, put them in a large pot and add water to cover. Bring to a boil then cover the pan and turn the heat off. After 20 minutes pour cold water on the eggs then remove them from the pan to cool.

Best Macaroni Salad

I love macaroni salad and I was on a mission to make the best one I could. It's even better made many hours or a day ahead.

2 cups uncooked pasta
4 hard-boiled eggs, chopped
4 green onions, sliced
4 ribs celery, chopped
5 sweet pickles, chopped
2 cups Miracle Whip or mayonnaise
1 - 4 ½ ounce can sliced black olives, rinsed and drained
3 tablespoons prepared mustard
2 tablespoons white sugar
2 ¼ teaspoons apple cider vinegar
¼ teaspoon salt
¾ teaspoon celery seed

Bring a large pot of water to a boil, add the noodles, put a lid on the pan and turn the heat off. Let it sit on the burner that has now been turned off for 20 minutes. Pour macaroni into colander, rinse well with cold water, add the macaroni and all other ingredients to a large bowl and stir until well mixed.

Perfect Italian Dressing

This does not need refrigeration. People will ask for this recipe!

⅔ cup olive oil (light, regular or extra-virgin all work)
¼ cup plus 2 tablespoons red wine vinegar
2 tablespoons white sugar
1 tablespoon prepared brown spicy mustard
2 - packages Italian dressing mix
⅔ cup seasoned rice wine vinegar
Black pepper to taste

Whisk all together and store in a glass bottle.

Great Greek Salad

This is best after a night in the refrigerator. Can be served old or room temperature.

½ cup olive oil (light, regular or extra-virgin all work)
½ cup red wine vinegar
2 teaspoons white sugar
1 ½ teaspoons dried basil
1 ½ teaspoons dried oregano
1 teaspoon black pepper
4 Roma tomatoes, chopped
2 red peppers, chopped
6 ounces feta cheese, crumbled
1 medium onion, chopped
2 handfuls Kalamata olives, rough chopped
Red pepper flakes to taste

Whisk oil, vinegar, sugar, basil, oregano, pepper and red pepper flakes. Add that to tomatoes, peppers, feta, onions and olives. Serve or chill overnight.

Curried Cole Slaw

One more gem from my mom! Even people who don't normally like raisins like this.

2 cups mayonnaise (or Miracle Whip)
2 tablespoons curry powder (or more if you like it spicy)
1 large head cabbage, shredded
1 ½ cups raisins
1 ½ cups Spanish peanuts, left whole
1 ½ cups frozen peas, thawed

Mix and serve. This is even good the next day.

Peanut Butter Pasta Salad

This is so creamy and it doesn't lose any seasoning after being in the refrigerator.

1 large head cauliflower, broken into small florets
1 pound uncooked radiatore, cavatappi or penne pasta
1 cup green onions, sliced thin
1 ½ cups peanut butter
¼ cup soy sauce
2 teaspoons sesame oil
¼ cup brown rice vinegar
½ cup Parmesan cheese, shredded (can also substitute nutritional yeast flakes from a natural food store)
2 tablespoons lemon juice
1 cup water
2 tablespoons honey
1 large red pepper, chopped small
1 - 8 ounce can sliced water chestnuts, rinsed and drained
Salt, red pepper flakes and hot sauce to taste

Bring a large pot of water to a boil, add the pasta and cauliflower, put a lid on the pan and turn the heat off. Let it sit on the burner that has now been turned off for 20 minutes. While that sits, in a large bowl mix together peanut butter, soy sauce, sesame oil, vinegar, lemon juice, water and honey until smooth. To that mixture add Parmesan, red pepper, green onions and water chestnuts then set aside. Drain pasta and cauliflower and toss well with the peanut butter mixture to coat. Add salt, red pepper flakes and hot sauce and serve room temperature or cold.

Creamy Salad Dressing

Not just for a lettuce salad, this is good on everything! I even dip bread in it.

1 cup mayonnaise
1 cup plus 2 tablespoons olive oil (light, regular or extra-virgin all work)
¾ cup plus 1 tablespoon red wine vinegar
1 ½ teaspoons garlic powder
1 ½ teaspoons dried oregano
1 ½ teaspoons dried basil
1 ¼ teaspoons black pepper
1 ¼ teaspoons salt
1 ¼ teaspoons onion powder
1 ¼ teaspoons Dijon mustard
2 tablespoons honey
½ teaspoon red pepper flakes

Mix all in a blender and store in the refrigerator.

Zesty Green Dressing

This is just as good on a salad as it is a dip for vegetables.

⅔ cup mayonnaise
Zest of 1 lemon (zest the lemon before you juice it)
2 teaspoons lemon juice
2 egg yolks
1 tablespoon white vinegar
1 teaspoon Worcestershire sauce
½ teaspoon dry mustard
½ teaspoon onion, minced
Black pepper to taste
Dash of hot sauce
Handful of fresh parsley

Put all in a blender and process until smooth. Store in the refrigerator.

Ranch Dressing

I made this up when I ran out of ranch and now we never buy it from the store.

1 cup mayonnaise
1 tablespoon plus 1 teaspoon lemon juice
½ cup liquid non-dairy creamer
1 teaspoon sugar
1 teaspoon salt
½ teaspoon dried chives
½ teaspoon garlic powder
¼ teaspoon dried parsley
¼ teaspoon onion powder
¼ teaspoon dry mustard
⅛ teaspoon dried dill weed
⅛ teaspoon paprika
⅛ teaspoon black pepper

Whisk all together and refrigerate 30 minutes before serving.

Taco Salad Dressing

This is from my sister Lynn and it is perfect on a salad for a Mexican meal.

1 cup mayonnaise
⅓ cup honey
½ cup red wine vinegar
¼ teaspoon garlic powder
½ teaspoon ground cumin

Whisk all together and refrigerate.

Taco Salad

I have been making this since I had it in my high school home economics class.

Iceberg lettuce, chopped, as much as you want
Tomatoes, chopped, as much as you want
Avocado, chopped, as much as you want
Hamburger, cooked and cooled, as much as you want
Kidney beans, rinsed and drained, as much as you want
Cheddar cheese, shredded, as much as you want
Hot sauce, as much as you want
Thousand Island salad dressing, as much as you want
Corn chips, crushed and spread over the top of the salad

Mix all together, add dressing and chips right before serving.

Sweet and Sour Dressing

This is wonderful on a lettuce salad and it also works for coleslaw too.

2 cups white sugar
1 ½ cups white vinegar
2 teaspoons fresh ginger, peeled and grated
2 tablespoons sesame oil
1 tablespoon lemon juice
1 ½ teaspoons salt
4 teaspoons dry mustard
2 tablespoons soy sauce
1 clove garlic, minced
4 tablespoons olive oil (light, regular or extra-virgin all work)
2 teaspoons black pepper

Whisk sugar, mustard and vinegar and cook over medium heat until sugar dissolves. Stir in soy sauce, ginger, garlic, oils, lemon juice, salt and pepper and blend well. Remove from heat and refrigerate at least four hours before serving. Shake well before use.

4

BREAD

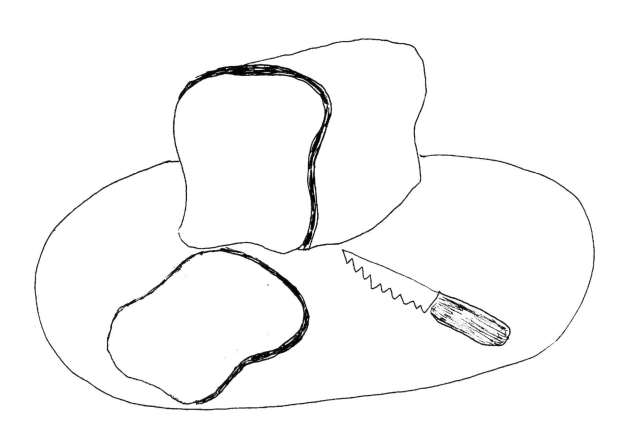

Buckaroo Bread

Heavy, dense bread that really stays with you. It is perfect for toast or sandwiches.

1 ½ cups warm water
1 package active dry yeast (or 2 teaspoons)
5 cups white spelt flour (or any flour you like)
5 tablespoons honey
½ teaspoon salt
2 pinches white sugar

Before you start, turn your oven to 170° (or lowest setting). Mix water, yeast and two pinches of sugar and let it sit for five minutes. In a large bowl, add flour, honey, salt and yeast mixture. Mix until it is combined, then turn it out on a floured surface. Turn the oven off. Knead the dough for 8 minutes then put it back in the bowl and let it rise in the oven for an hour. After an hour, punch the dough down and shape into a loaf and put it in a loaf pan that has been well sprayed with cooking spray and let it rise again for 45 minutes. Bake at 350° for 35-40 minutes. When it is done, it will sound hollow when tapped on the top. I slice it after it cools and I keep the slices in our freezer. It must be stored in the refrigerator or freezer.

Upper Crust Oat Bread

Slightly sweet, you can really taste the oats and it is so good for you too! When you cool the loaf, set it on its side on a wire cooling rack. The indentations it leaves will make a perfect slicing guide.

1 ½ cups warm water
1 package active dry yeast (or 2 teaspoons)
3 cups white spelt flour (or any flour you like)
2 cups oats, mixed in a blender until it is flour (quick or old-fashioned)
5 tablespoons honey
½ teaspoon salt
2 big pinches white sugar

Before you start, turn your oven to 170° (or lowest setting). Mix water, yeast and white sugar together and let it sit for 5 minutes. In a large bowl, add flour, oats, honey, salt and yeast mixture. Mix until it is combined, scraping the bowl to get all the flour then turn it out on a floured surface. Turn the oven off. Place dough on lightly floured surface and knead for 8 minutes, then put it back in the bowl and let it rise in the oven for an hour. After an hour, punch the dough down and shape into a loaf and put it in a loaf pan that has been well sprayed with cooking spray and let it rise again for 45 minutes. Bake in preheated 350° oven for 40-45 minutes. When it is done, it will sound hollow when tapped on the top. I slice it after it is cooled and I keep the slices in our freezer. It must be stored in the refrigerator or freezer.

Iowa Cornbread

I like to make croutons with this cornbread on the rare occasion there's any left.

Take any boxed cornbread mix and make as the package suggests. Then add a can of creamed corn and bake it as the package recommends. You will end up with the moistest cornbread you've ever had and it will last for days in the refrigerator and be just as moist.

Green Apple Bread

Try this with egg salad sandwiches - yum! It's amazing toasted and you'll always want a sliced loaf in your freezer.

1 package active dry yeast (or 2 teaspoons)
3 tablespoons white sugar
1 cup warm water
2 eggs, room temperature
½ teaspoon vanilla extract
1 teaspoon salt
4 cups flour
3 cups green apples, diced small

Before you start, turn your oven to 170° (or lowest setting). Pour ½ cup warm water into the bowl of a large food processor. Add yeast and sugar and mix a few seconds then let stand for 5 minutes. Mix in remaining water, eggs, salt and vanilla. Add flour a cup at a time, mixing after each addition. You may or may not need to add an additional cup of flour to make it the right. Turn the oven off. Take dough out of the processor and onto a lightly floured surface and knead in the apples. Place dough in an oiled bowl and let rise 1 ½ hours in the oven. Punch the dough down, divide it in two and let rise 30 minutes in two loaf pans that have been sprayed with cooking spray. Bake at 375° for 35 minutes or until they are golden brown. Let cool before slicing. *You can also mix this by hand if you don't have a food processor.

Butternut Squash Bread

This bread is delicious with the most beautiful color thanks to the squash. We use it for sandwiches and for toast too.

2 packages active dry yeast (or 4 teaspoons)
½ cup warm water
1 ¼ cups butternut squash, roasted then blended until smooth
1 cup warm milk
2 eggs, beaten
Pinch of white sugar
⅓ cup butter, melted
3 tablespoons honey
1 teaspoon salt
7 cups flour (plus up to ½ cup more as you knead)

Preheat oven to 450°. Cut squash in half, lay both halves on a baking sheet that has been oiled. Bake for 40 minutes then remove and let cool. When the squash is cool enough to handle, scoop the flesh into a bowl, mash well then set aside. In a small bowl, dissolve yeast in water, add a pinch of sugar then let stand for 5 minutes. Heat milk with butter until butter is melted. In large bowl combine squash, milk mixture, eggs, honey and salt; mix well. Add 5 cups flour and mix until smooth. Add two more cups of flour to form a soft dough then turn onto a lightly floured surface and knead for 8 minutes. Add more flour as needed so it does not stick. Place in a greased bowl. Cover and let rise for an hour in the warmed oven you used to cook the squash in. Punch dough down. Shape into two loaves and place in greased loaf pans. Cover and let rise 30 minutes. Bake at 375° for 30 minutes. Remove from pans to cool. The bread is easier to cut when it has cooled down and it must be stored in the refrigerator.

Pizza Dough

This is a no wait, no knead, super quick pizza dough.

3 cups flour
1 cup warm water
1 package active dry yeast (or 2 teaspoons)
2 tablespoons olive oil (light, regular or extra-virgin all work)
1 teaspoon salt
1 tablespoon white sugar
1 tablespoon dried basil
1 tablespoon dried oregano

Combine flour, salt, sugar, and yeast in a large bowl. Mix in oil and warm water. It will seem a bit dry but just knead the dough and it will come together. Spray pan heavily. Roll out dough then transfer to a 16-inch pizza pan (I like the kind with holes in the pan). Top as desired. Bake at 450° until done – about 25 minutes. We like thin crust so with the extra dough I make bread sticks sprinkled with Parmesan and I bake them at 450° for about 20 minutes, or longer if you like them more crispy.

Homemade Flour Tortilla's

So much better than store bought! They harden in the fridge so soften them in a warm oven for a few minutes before using. Makes 8 tortillas so I often double the recipe.

2 cups flour
¼ cup shortening (I use coconut oil – in the healthy food section)
⅔ cup warm water
¼ teaspoon salt (optional)

Preheat your oven to its lowest setting. If you have a food processor, add four, salt and shortening to the bowl. Pulse until it is mixed then slowly stream in water and process until a dough forms. If you do not have a food processor, mix the flour and salt together then cut the shortening in until it is in small pieces. Add the water and mix until the dough comes together. The dough will be sticky, so turn it onto a well floured surface and knead until it comes together and is smooth. Divide dough in half, then from each half, cut 4 equal portions and let them rest on the counter for 30 minutes. Heat a dry cast iron pan over medium-high heat. On a well floured surface, roll out each ball of dough as large and as thin as you can; the thinner, the better. Place them on the pan (I use a cast iron pizza pan), one at a time for about 30 seconds then flip over once bubbles start to form. I pop the bubbles with my tongs before I flip them. Keep the tortillas in a warm oven while you cook the rest. Sweet topping ideas: 1) Softened butter, lemon or orange zest and honey. 2) Softened butter, cinnamon and white sugar. 3) Softened cream cheese, your favorite pie filling, cinnamon and white sugar.

Peanut Butter Bread

There are few things better than toasted peanut butter bread. This is heavy and does not rise too much so it makes a very dense loaf. When measuring sticky substances, lightly oil the measuring cup first and the sticky substance will just fall out.

3 cups flour
1 cup warm water
1 tablespoon white sugar
1 package active dry yeast (or 2 teaspoons)
2 tablespoons honey
1 teaspoon salt
1 tablespoon brown sugar, firmly packed
1 cup peanut butter
1 tablespoon olive oil (light, regular or extra-virgin all work)
1 egg

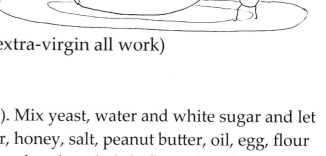

Turn your oven to 170° (or lowest setting). Mix yeast, water and white sugar and let it sit for 5 minutes. Combine brown sugar, honey, salt, peanut butter, oil, egg, flour and yeast mixture. Turn the oven off. Place dough on lightly floured surface and knead for 6 minutes. Place in a well greased pan and let rise for two hours in a warm place. Bake at 350° for 40 minutes.

Buckle Up Biscuits

I cannot tell you how many times I tried to make the perfect biscuit until I perfected this recipe. This is the King of Biscuits; fluffy pillows of pure goodness that are impossible to mess up. They will come out perfectly every single time.

4 cups Bisquick baking mix
1 cup sour cream
6 ounces lemon-lime soft drink or beer (If you halve the recipe you'll need ⅓ cup)

Preheat oven to 400°. Mix the sour cream into the Bisquick mix with a fork until it is crumbly. Add soft drink or beer and mix until just incorporated. Turn out onto a lightly floured surface and quickly knead 8 times to bring the dough together. Then separate dough in two pieces. Pat into two separate rectangles on a baking sheet and cut through the dough on each rectangle in 6 pieces keeping the biscuits still attached to each other. Bake 20 minutes exactly.

Cinnamon Rusk

I had these as a child and I hope it brings back a lot of wonderful memories for you too! If the dough seems dry, add a splash or two more of milk so it can come together and be kneaded. Keep in mind these take two days to make but they're worth it!

4 cups flour
6 tablespoons sugar
2 ½ teaspoons yeast (1 ½ packets)
Big pinch of salt
½ teaspoon ground cinnamon
¼ teaspoon ground nutmeg
4 tablespoons unsalted butter; melted, then set aside
1 large egg
1 cup milk, room temperature
Ground cinnamon-white sugar mixture (you decide the ratio)
Olive oil to grease the bowl

Turn your oven on to the lowest temperature you can for a few minutes then turn the heat off. Combine all of the ingredients (except the cinnamon-sugar mixture), mix and knead to form a smooth, somewhat sticky dough. Put the dough in the oven in a bowl that has been greased with olive oil and let it rise two hours. Divide it in half and shape each half into a 12-inch log then put them on a parchment-lined baking sheet. Put it back in the oven and let it rise for 90 more minutes. Take the bread out (the loaves will be sort of flattened) and preheat the oven to 350°. Bake the bread for 24 minutes then remove from the oven and let it sit out at room temperature overnight. The next day, cut the loaves into ½-inch slices. Lay them on ungreased baking sheets and bake at 200° for one hour. Flip the pieces over and sprinkle each generously with the cinnamon-sugar mixture. Return them to the oven and bake for one hour and 15 minutes more then remove from the oven and cool completely. Store in an air tight container at room temperature.

Lemon Drizzle Bread

A tasty treat that comes from England. It is very moist and if you love lemon, this is for you!

1 ½ cups flour
1 cup butter, softened
2 ¼ cups powdered sugar plus 6 tablespoons
4 eggs
Juice and zest of 2 lemons (zest the lemons before you juice them)

Preheat oven to 350°. Beat butter and two cups powdered sugar until creamy. Add eggs. Mix in flour and zest. Spray a large loaf pan with cooking spray then add batter and level the top. Bake 45-50 minutes. While that is cooking, whisk the lemon juice with 6 tablespoons of powdered sugar and set aside. When the cake comes out of the oven, poke it all over with a skewer then pour the juice/sugar mixture evenly over the top.

47

Orange Cranberry Bread

My husband's mom made this every Christmas and they would devour many loaves! We now eat it all year round. It is moist, dense and simply delicious!

2 cups flour
1 cup white sugar
1 ½ teaspoons baking powder
½ teaspoon baking soda
1 teaspoon salt
1 egg
2 tablespoons melted butter
Juice and zest of 1 orange
Boiling water (as needed)
1 cup walnuts or pecans, chopped
1 cup fresh cranberries, halved

Preheat oven to 350°. Mix flour, sugar, baking powder, soda and salt together and set aside. In another bowl, combine the orange juice, orange zest, melted butter *and only if needed,* enough boiling water to make a total of ¾ cup. Add beaten egg to juice mixture then add that to the dry ingredients and stir until just mixed. Do not over mix or it will collapse in the center and not cook right. Mix in the nuts and cranberries and pour into a well greased loaf pan, pushing batter into the corners. Bake for 60 minutes. Cover with foil the last 10 minutes of baking so top doesn't get too brown. Cool loaf before removing from pan. Makes one medium sized loaf.

```
               Food Fact:
   Cranberries are sorted for ripeness by bouncing them.
 A fully ripened cranberry can be dribbled like a basketball.
```

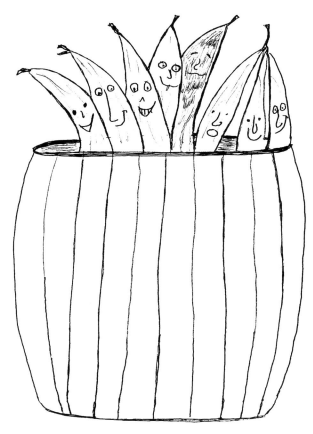

Barrel of Bananas Bread

This is the BEST banana bread because it is packed with extra bananas!

2 cups flour
1 teaspoon baking soda
¼ teaspoon salt
½ cup butter, softened
¾ cup brown sugar, firmly packed
2 eggs, beaten
6 ripe bananas

Preheat oven to 350°. Grease a loaf pan. In a large bowl, combine flour, salt, and baking soda. In a separate bowl, cream butter and brown sugar then stir in the eggs. Add the flour mixture. Mash 5 of the bananas and add them to the batter. Dice the last banana then gently fold that in until the batter is just moistened. Lumps are ok. Don't over mix it or it'll be gummy in the middle after you bake it. Bake for 55 minutes. Let it cool in the pan for 15 minutes then take it out and cool it to room temperature or it will crumble when sliced. *If using two smaller loaf pans, bake them for 40 minutes.

Amish Friendship Bread

Do not use metal spoons or bowl for mixing. Do not refrigerate. If air gets into the bag, let it out. It is normal for the batter to bubble and ferment. If you have never tried this, you will be a fan soon!

Day 1: Do nothing. This is the day you got the bag.
Day 2: Squish the bag
Day 3: Squish the bag
Day 4: Squish the bag
Day 5: Squish the bag
Day 6: Add to the bag: 1 cup flour, 1 cup sugar, 1 cup milk, then squish the bag.
Day 7: Squish the bag
Day 8: Squish the bag
Day 9: Squish the bag
Day 10: Baking Day!
On baking day, preheat oven to 325°. Pour contents of bag into large bowl and add: 1 ½ cups flour, 1 ½ cups sugar and 1 ½ cups milk. Put one cup of batter into four zip-top gallon bags. Keep one and give the others to friends with the recipe.

To the remaining batter you have in your bowl after dividing the 3 cups out add:
3 eggs
1 cup oil, olive or canola
1 cup milk
1 cup white sugar
2 teaspoons ground cinnamon
½ teaspoon vanilla
1½ teaspoons baking powder
½ teaspoon baking soda
½ teaspoon salt
2 cups flour
2 - 3.4 ounce boxes of instant pudding, any flavor
Cinnamon/sugar mixture: ½ cup white sugar; 1 ½ teaspoons ground cinnamon

Butter two large loaf pans. Dust with half the cinnamon/sugar mixture. Pour batter evenly into the pans and sprinkle with remaining cinnamon/sugar mix. Bake for one hour. Cool until bread loosens from sides of pan.

Amish Friendship Bread Starter

Thanks to my neighbor Katrina, this is the start of one of the best sweet breads you will ever have! Use this in my Amish Friendship Bread recipe.

1 package active dry yeast (or 2 teaspoons)
¼ cup warm water
3 cups flour, divided
3 cups white sugar, divided
3 cups milk

In a small bowl, dissolve yeast in water. Let stand 10 minutes. In a two quart non metal container, combine one cup flour and one cup sugar. Mix well or flour will lump when milk is added. Slowly stir in one cup milk and yeast mixture. Cover loosely and let stand until bubbly. This is day one. Leave this starter loosely covered at room temperature. On days 2 thru 4; stir starter. Day 5; stir in one cup flour, one cup sugar and one cup milk. Days 6 thru 9; stir only. Day 10; stir in one cup flour, one cup sugar and one cup milk. Remove one cup to make your first bread, give two cups to friends along with the Amish Bread recipe. Either store the remaining one cup starter in the refrigerator, or begin the 10 day process over again.
*Once you have made the starter, consider it Day 1, and thus ignore step 1 in this recipe and proceed with step 2. You can also freeze the starter in one cup measures but it takes at least three hours at room temperature to thaw.

Food Fact:
Horatio Spatula immigrated to the United States in the 1880s. One day he attempted to flip his fried eggs with a broom stick and when that didn't work, his wife handed him a coal-scuttle (small bucket that held coal). He eventually cut the bucket in half, then reduced it even more, making something that resembled the spatula that we know today.

5

SOUP

Bursting Black Bean Soup

Not too spicy and it is so creamy once it takes a spin in the blender.

2 cups vegetable or chicken stock
¾ cup black beans, rinsed, drained and reserve half of them
¾ cup chickpeas, rinsed, drained and reserve half of them
Half a jalapeno pepper, seeds removed
¼ cup red pepper, diced
1 green onion, sliced
½ cup canned diced tomatoes
2 tablespoons lime juice
½ teaspoon ground cumin
2 teaspoons chili powder
1 teaspoon soy sauce
2 teaspoons Worcestershire sauce
1 teaspoon hot sauce

If you have a high speed blender (I like Vitamix or Blendtec), toss all of the ingredients in that and mix on high for 8 minutes to get steaming hot soup. Then add the reserved black beans and chickpeas; blend 10 seconds more. If you do not have a high speed blender, puree all the ingredients in a blender then heat soup in a sauce pan. As it is heating, puree the reserved black beans and chick peas in the blender for 10 seconds then add them to the soup.

Buttermilk Broccoli Cheese Bisque

There is no better way to get kids to eat broccoli than by adding cheese. This soup is smooth and creamy and something we have often!

2 cups buttermilk (or any kind of milk you have)
½ cup dry potato flakes (*or* one medium cooked potato, cubed *or* a few big spoons of prepared mashed potatoes)
1 cup Velveeta cheese, small cubes
1 cup sharp Cheddar cheese, small cubes
¼ cup sour cream
2 heaping cups broccoli, steamed
2 tablespoons onion, chopped
2 teaspoons cornstarch
½ teaspoon concentrated vegetable stock base (or one bouillon cube)
2 teaspoons Worcestershire sauce
1 teaspoon soy sauce
Pinch red pepper flakes
Hot sauce to taste

I use a high speed blender (I like Vitamix or Blendtec) to make this. Just blend for 8 minutes to get hot soup. Don't worry if the top of the soup is not moving in your high speed blender, it will in time. If you don't have a high speed blender, you can process the mixture in a blender then heat it up in a pan.

```
                          Food Fact:
      The word "soup" comes from the Middle Ages word "sop,"
       which means a slice of bread over which roast drippings
    were poured. The first evidence of soup being consumed dates
          back thousands of years and the main ingredient was
                        hippopotamus bones.
```

Cowgirl Corn Chowder

Hearty and delicious served with a crusty load of rustic bread, slathered with butter.

6 red potatoes, cut in bite sized cubes
2 - 11 ounce cans of corn and their juice (or 2 cups fresh corn kernels)
2 carrots, small dice
½ cup onion, small dice
½ cup parsley, chopped
4 cups vegetable or chicken stock
Red pepper flakes to taste

Add all to a soup pot. Cook until the vegetables are tender but not mushy.

Hearty Carrot Soup

Simple and easy comfort food. This reheats very well the next day.

2 tablespoons olive oil (light, regular or extra-virgin all work)
2 small onions, chopped
2 teaspoons coriander seeds, crushed
2 pounds carrots, sliced
6 cups vegetable stock
2 cups cilantro, packed full & chopped
Salt and hot sauce to taste

In a large soup pot over medium heat, cook onion and coriander seeds in oil, about 5 minutes, stirring occasionally. Add carrots. Cook, covered, until softened, 15-20 minutes, stirring occasionally. In a separate pot, bring stock to a boil. Add onion-carrot mixture and bring back up to a boil. Transfer to a blender or food processor and blend in batches, until it is smooth. Serve immediately.

Cheesy Hash Brown Soup

This soup is amazing and a product of a lot of testing until I got it just right. You can also add cooked ground beef to this to make delicious cheesy ground beef soup.

6 cups water
2 - 10 ¾ ounce cans cream of celery soup
30 ounce package hash browns, thawed
2 celery stalks, diced
1 medium onion, diced
3 carrots, diced
32 ounce package Velveeta cheese, diced
Salt and pepper to taste
1 teaspoon Worcestershire sauce
2 tablespoons soy sauce
Crispy crumbled bacon and sliced green onions for garnish (optional)

Add carrots, celery and onion to large soup pot. Then add water, hash browns and celery soup. Bring to a boil. Once the water is boiling, add the Velveeta. Lower the heat and stir occasionally until cheese is melted and soup is creamy and heated through. Top each bowl full with crispy bits of bacon and sliced green onions if desired. This freezes well too.

```
Food Fact:
Apples are more effective than caffeine at waking you up
in the morning.
```

Terrific Tomato Soup

Try this piping hot with my Nashville Dilled Cheese Sandwich on a cold winter day! My husband likes to crumble graham crackers on top of his. Something he grew up doing that I have come to like too.

4 tablespoons butter
⅛ cup flour
1 ½ cups milk (I often use oat milk for the extra flavor it gives the soup)
46 ounces tomato juice
1 - 15 ounce can tomato sauce
1 cup half-and-half
1 cup vegetable or chicken broth
¼ teaspoon baking soda
4 tablespoons honey
½ teaspoon salt
Black pepper to taste
Few pinches of red pepper flakes

Whisk butter and flour in soup pot and stir constantly, cooking on medium for two minutes. Lower the heat and add tomato juice, broth, milk, half-and-half, baking soda, honey and salt and heat through. Serve with crackers crushed on top if desired.

Triple Cheese Potato Soup

One of the Top 5 best soups I've ever had!

4 cups potatoes, skins on, small dice (I like red or Yukon Gold)
1 medium onion, small dice
1 cup carrots, small dice
½ cup celery, small dice
4 cups vegetable or chicken stock
½ cup butter
¼ cup flour
2 cups milk
½ pound sharp Cheddar cheese, in small cubes
½ pound pepper jack cheese, in small cubes
½ pound Velveeta cheese, in small cubes
Black pepper to taste

Place all of the vegetables and stock into a large soup pot. Bring to a boil and simmer for two minutes. In another pan, melt butter on medium-high, then lower heat to medium, add flour and cook one minute, whisking frequently. Add milk and whisk until smooth. Let it thicken for a few minutes then add the cheese and whisk until melted. When the vegetables are done, add cheese sauce to the pot and season with pepper. Serve immediately. To reheat; cook on low or the soup will scorch and the cheese won't fully melt. The next day to change it up, I add a handful of fresh corn kernels and a few big spoonfuls of canned, diced green chilies and I blend it in a high speed blender (I like Vitamix or Blendtec) on high for 8 minutes. If you don't have a high speed blender, process the cold soup in a blender and heat it up on low in a pan.

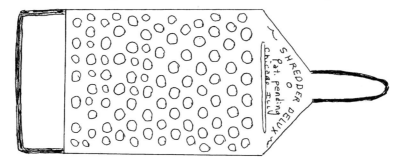

6

MAIN DISHES

Fall Off the Bone Chicken

The meat just falls off the bones and the sauce can be used as gravy.

1 – 4 or 5 pound whole chicken
1 ½ cups prepared barbecue sauce
¼ cup water

Put chicken, legs up, into crock pot. Pour sauce inside and over the chicken. Cover and cook 8 to 10 hours on low. Do not remove the lid to check it as it cooks.

Mr. Wren's Hen Bake

I grew up on this and I added the lemon to give it that something special.

3 boneless chicken breasts, skinned
1 - 10 ¾ ounce can cream of mushroom soup
1 teaspoon lemon juice
1 ½ cups mushrooms, chopped
1 small onion, chopped
Salt and black pepper to taste

Arrange chicken in a large baking dish. Combine soup, lemon juice, onion, mushrooms, salt and pepper; mix well. Spread evenly on chicken. Bake at 350° for one hour.

Gorgonzola Port Chicken and Pasta

This makes four servings and the color is beautiful! The taste is unlike anything you have ever had and it is one recipe you will serve often!

4 chicken breasts, marinated an hour in olive oil & garlic to taste
2 tablespoons butter
5 cups port wine
10 ounces Gorgonzola cheese, crumbled
1 ½ cups half & half
¼ cup parsley, chopped
1 pound and a half of uncooked pasta (I like penne best)
Red grapes, halved & soaked in all day in port wine, the more the better
Salt and black pepper to taste

Grill the chicken until it is done, then set aside, keeping it warm in the oven. Add butter to port wine to a medium sized pot & reduce the mixture by half. To reduce, just simmer or boil it until you think there is half as much liquid as there was in the beginning. I often judge this by looking at the sides of my pan when I start then when it is half of that, it is ready. It usually leaves a line where the liquid was when it started. After the butter/port mixture is reduced, add cream and 8 ounces of Gorgonzola & then reduce the entire mixture by half again. Bring a large pot of water to a boil, add noodles, put a lid on the pan and turn the heat off. Let it sit on the burner that has now been turned off for 20 minutes. Then drain and set aside. Toss the port/cheese mixture with hot pasta. To serve, add a big spoonful of pasta to a dinner plate, then top that with one chicken breast. To serve, sprinkle each breast with parsley, port soaked grapes and a few crumbles of Gorgonzola cheese.

Food fact:

Fried chicken is the most popular meal ordered in sit-down restaurants in the U.S. When making fried chicken, drain it on a wire rack, not paper towels, or your chicken will be soggy.

Day Ahead Fried Chicken

Just the right crunch for fried chicken perfection. This takes two days to make.

3 pounds chicken pieces
2 packages Italian salad dressing mix
3 tablespoons flour
2 teaspoons Old Bay seasoning
¼ cup lemon juice
1 ½ cups prepared pancake mix
1 teaspoon paprika
¼ teaspoon black pepper
Vegetable oil for frying

Mix chicken with Italian dressing mix, flour, Old Bay and lemon juice then cover and refrigerate overnight. The next day, mix pancake mix, paprika and pepper and put in a plastic bag. Add chicken and shake well. Dust off excess and put in the refrigerator for two hours. After two hours, put ¼-inch of oil in a frying pan and brown chicken for four minutes on each side. Place all pieces on a baking sheet, cover with foil and bake 45 minutes at 350°. Then turn oven to 400°, uncover and bake 10 minutes longer.

 # Kid-Loving Tenders

Thanks to my sister Amy! These are moist and tender with a crunchy coating. It works for fish too.

½ cup mayonnaise
¼ cup Parmesan cheese, grated
1 package boneless, skinless chicken breast or tenders
Bread crumbs (I prefer Panko bread crumbs)
Old Bay seasoning to taste

Preheat oven to 425°. Mix mayonnaise and Parmesan then spread on the chicken. Roll in bread crumbs seasoned with Old Bay and bake for 20 minutes.

Spicy Coconut Chicken Curry

Spicy

You know it is good and spicy when it makes your nose run!

X

3 skinless, boneless chicken breasts, cut in bite-size pieces
3 tablespoons olive oil (light, regular or extra-virgin all work)
1 small onion, chopped
2 cloves garlic, minced
3 tablespoons curry powder
1 teaspoon paprika
¾ teaspoon ground ginger
1 teaspoon chili powder
½ teaspoon white sugar
1 tablespoon tomato paste
1 cup plain yogurt
¾ cup coconut milk
Half a lemon, juiced
¼ teaspoon cayenne pepper
Pinch of salt

Cook onion in oil till tender, stir occasionally. Add to that the garlic, cur[...]
paprika, chili powder, ginger, sugar and salt. Cook for two minutes, stirring
constantly. Add chicken, tomato paste, yogurt and coconut milk. Bring to a
boil, reduce heat and simmer 25 minutes. Remove bay leaf and stir in lemon
juice and cayenne. Simmer 5 minutes then serve on jasmine rice if you have it
or any rice will do.

```
                          Food Fact:
     An average woman consumes approximately 44 pounds of
                   lipstick in her lifetime.
```

Buffalo Wing Dings

These are so good and they're wonderful served with my Blue Cheese Ranch Dip.

20 chicken wings
½ cup butter
¾ cup hot sauce
1 teaspoon garlic, minced
1 cup flour
½ teaspoon paprika
½ teaspoon cayenne pepper
½ teaspoon onion powder
¼ teaspoon salt
Pinch of black pepper

Combine butter, hot sauce, pepper and garlic over low heat until melted. Set aside. In a bowl mix flour, paprika, cayenne, salt and onion powder. Place wings in a large bowl and toss with flour mixture. Place chicken in shallow baking dish and cover them evenly with the remaining flour mixture then cover and refrigerate two hours; do not miss this step! After two hours, put wings on parchment paper or on a wire rack on a jelly roll pan and bake at 350° for 45-55 minutes. Then turn oven to 375°, spray wings with cooking spray and bake 5-10 minutes longer. Toss them in the butter sauce right when they come out of the oven and serve.

Chicken Supream

I grew up eating this often. It was one of my mom's specialties! When I make it now, I sometimes double the sauce because it is so incredible.

2 ½ to 3 pounds chicken, cut into serving pieces
2 tablespoons butter, melted
1 teaspoon salt
¼ teaspoon pepper
¾ cup non dairy powdered coffee creamer
1 tablespoon flour
1 - 4 ounce can mushroom pieces and their liquid
1 teaspoon paprika
1 teaspoon Worcestershire sauce

Place chicken in shallow baking dish. Brush with melted butter then sprinkle with salt and pepper. Bake at 400° for 45 minutes. Drain mushrooms; measure liquid; adding water to make ¾ cup. In mixing bowl make a sauce with powdered coffee creamer, flour, mushroom liquid, paprika and Worcestershire sauce. Whisk until blended. Add mushrooms pieces. Spoon over chicken and continue baking 10-15 minutes longer. Serve over rice.

```
                        Food Fact:
This recipe is from the late 60's and it is no longer around
 because Pream non-dairy powdered creamer is not being made
any more. My mom still had the original recipe torn out of a
magazine and I got permission from the company that owns the
  Pream name to include this in my cookbook. It is a classic
    recipe that you can't even locate by doing a search on
      Google. This is the only place you will find it!
```

Overnight Turkey

This is from my brother-in-law Tim and it is for a 20 pound turkey which takes about 16 hours to cook. It cannot be stuffed. The best part is your whole house smells like turkey when you wake up.

1 - 20 pound turkey
2 tablespoons black pepper
2 tablespoons seasoning salt
2 tablespoons lemon pepper seasoning
2 tablespoons garlic powder
2 tablespoons paprika
2 tablespoons onion powder
1 teaspoon cayenne pepper
1 tablespoon salt
Olive oil (light, regular or extra-virgin all work)

Before you go to bed, preheat oven to 400°. Rinse your turkey inside and out, remove giblets and pat dry. Sprinkle the inside of the turkey's cavity with one tablespoon of salt. Rub the outside of the turkey with olive oil. Mix together pepper, seasoning salt, lemon pepper, garlic powder, paprika, onion powder and cayenne then sprinkle it over the top of the turkey. Cover turkey roaster with a lid, bake at 400° for one hour then turn the oven down to 195°, do not open the oven door, leaving it cook overnight. Check the internal temperature a few hours before eating. If it has not reached 185°, turn the oven up to 350° until it is done. The turkey doesn't look pretty when it is done, but it is moist and tender and juicy.

Squat and Gobble Turkey

This sounds like it can't work but try it! It is the only way to cook a smaller turkey.

1 - 12 pound turkey, thawed, with the giblets removed
½ cup butter, melted
Half of a lemon or lime
Half of an orange
Half of a small red onion,
1 stalk celery, cut in pieces
1 medium carrot, cut in pieces
2 cups boiling water
Salt and black pepper to taste

Preheat oven to 500°. Take giblets out of the turkey, pour butter all over the outside of the turkey then sprinkle it with salt and pepper. Put celery, onion, lemon or lime, orange and carrot inside the cavity and place the turkey, breast side up, in a large roasting pan with a tight fitting lid. Pour boiling water into pan. Cover it and put in oven for one hour. Then turn off the oven off, leaving the turkey inside and do not open the oven door for the next 5 hours. Do not sneak a peek! When 5 hours is up, the turkey will be done and it will have the most amazing color and it will be the most tender turkey you've ever tasted. The largest bird you can safely cook this way is 12 pounds or under. Get one as close to 12 pounds as you can. *Another way you can vary this recipe is to cook the bird breast side down. The white meat will be a little bit moister, but it won't look as good when it's done.

Food Fact:
A spooked turkey can run at speeds up to 20 miles per hour.
They can also burst into flight approaching speeds between
50-55 miles per hour in a matter of seconds.

Tender Turkey Burgers

My beef loving husband really likes these. They are very moist and flavorful and this recipe makes 6 extra-large burgers.

2 pounds ground turkey (I like a mixture of light and dark meat)
1 large onion, finely chopped
1 egg
2 teaspoons olive oil (light, regular or extra-virgin all work)
1 cup bread crumbs
2 teaspoons soy sauce
2 teaspoons Worcestershire sauce
1 tablespoon dried parsley
1 teaspoon garlic powder
1 teaspoon spicy brown mustard
1 teaspoon black pepper
1 teaspoon poultry seasoning
Dash of salt

Combine all ingredients in a large bowl and mix just until combined. Shape into 6 patties then refrigerate for 20 minutes before cooking. Cook over medium heat for four minutes each side. You can also bake them at 400° for 20 minutes.

Cattle Call Meatloaf

Meatloaf gets no respect but this one will have everyone singing its praises! It is so moist and just as good cold the next day.

2 pounds extra-lean ground beef
1 tablespoon butter
¼ cup onion, minced
2 cloves garlic, minced
1 ½ teaspoons salt
1 ½ teaspoons black pepper
3 slices bread, toasted and roughly crumbled
7 Ritz or soda crackers, crushed
1 egg, lightly beaten
3 ½ tablespoons sour cream
1 ½ tablespoons Worcestershire sauce
1 - 15 ounce can tomato sauce, divided
3 tablespoons ketchup

Preheat oven to 350°. Melt the butter in a skillet and cook the onion and garlic for 5 minutes. Remove from heat and season with salt and pepper. In a large bowl, combine the onion mixture with the beef, bread, crackers, sour cream, egg, Worcestershire and ½ can tomato sauce. Transfer to a loaf pan and b uncovered 40 minutes. You will then need to remove it from the oven and carefully drain off the excess liquid using a turkey baster. Increase oven to 400°and bake 15 minutes more, then remove any more liquid. In a small bowl, mix the remaining tomato sauce and ketchup, pour that over the top of the meatloaf and bake it 10 minutes longer.

Food Fact:
In an effort to boost sales of catsup in the 1830s,
one manufacturer bottled it as 'Dr. Miles Compound Extract
of Tomato,' said to cure anything from baldness to athletes
foot to everything in-between.

Delicious Cheese Beef Buns

We often add dill pickle slices to these and the sky is the limit as to what you can add!

4 ½ cups flour
¼ cup white sugar
4 teaspoons active dry yeast
1 teaspoon salt
¾ cup milk
½ cup water
½ cup shortening (I use coconut oil from a health food store)
2 eggs, beaten slightly

Filling:
1 pound lean ground beef
1 medium onion, chopped
1 tablespoon dried parsley
1 teaspoon dry mustard
1 ½ teaspoons garlic, minced
1 teaspoon salt
½ teaspoon black pepper
Shredded cheese, any kind and as much as you want
Prepared mustard, as much as you want

In a large bowl, place 1 ¾ cups flour, sugar, yeast and salt. Heat milk, water and shortening to between 120° and 130°. Pour that over flour mixture and add the eggs. Beat on low until blended then beat on high for 3 minutes. Stir in the remaining 2 ¾ cups flour, pour onto floured work surface and knead dough for 5 minutes. Place dough in a greased bowl; cover and let rise in a warm place for an hour. As that rises, brown beef, onions, salt and pepper in a skillet. Punch dough down; roll into 12 or 14 thin rectangles. Top half of each with ¾ cup meat mixture, a squirt of mustard and shredded cheese. Fold the other half over the meat mixture and pinch the edges all the way around to seal so nothing leaks out. Place on a greased baking sheet and bake at 350° until golden brown, about 25-35 minutes.

Canteen Slim's Flank Steak

This also works for meat, poultry and fish. The longer you marinate it, the better.

1 ½ pounds of flank steak
½ cup soy sauce
2 tablespoons brown sugar, firmly packed
2 tablespoons lemon juice
2 tablespoons olive oil (light, regular or extra-virgin all work)
2 cloves garlic, minced
1 tablespoon onion, minced
1 teaspoon ground ginger
½ teaspoon black pepper

Whisk all together and pour over meat that you have placed in a zip closure gallon plastic bag. I then put that in another bag in case one leaks. Marinate in the fridge for 2-3 days. Flip the bag over in the refrigerator a few times every day. You can cook this on a grill or broil it in the oven.

Steak Sauce

Better than store bought! This keeps for a long time in the fridge.

1 cup ketchup
½ cup onion, coarsely chopped
1 large clove garlic, chopped in large pieces
¼ cup water
2 tablespoons Worcestershire sauce
¼ cup lemon juice
¼ cup white vinegar
2 tablespoons brown sugar, firmly packed
1 tablespoon prepared mustard
Salt to taste
Dash of hot sauce

Combine all ingredients in a small pan and simmer uncovered for 30 minutes, stirring occasionally. Strain to remove onion and garlic then cool and store in refrigerator.

Plate Scrapin' Meatballs

Cooking this all day gives it incredible flavor! It couldn't be easier either.

1 pound ground beef
1 cup bread crumbs
¼ cup parsley, chopped
2 cloves garlic, minced
1 medium yellow onion, chopped
1 egg, beaten
1 - 1 pound 16 ounce jar prepared spaghetti sauce
2 - 4 ounce cans mushrooms
1 - 14.5 ounce can diced tomatoes
1 - 14.5 ounce can tomato sauce
1 - 6 ounce can tomato paste
1 tablespoon dried basil
½ teaspoon dried oregano
½ teaspoon dried marjoram

In a bowl, mix beef, bread crumbs, parsley, garlic, onion and egg. Shape into meatballs. Add everything else to the crock pot, put meatballs on top and cook on low for 6-8 hours.

Food Fact:
A typical American eats 28 pigs in their lifetime.

Splatter Free Bacon

You will never fry bacon in a pan again with this no mess, no splattering, non greasy method.

Line baking sheet with foil, add bacon and put in a cold oven. Turn the oven to 400° and bake 12-15 minutes, depending on how crispy you like it.

South Dakota Beef Stew

I was born in Watertown, South Dakota and my grandma lived there most of her life. As of this publication she is still there and doing great at 95 years old. She used to make this all the time. I absolutely love the tang the lemon gives it and the biscuit topping makes this unforgettable!

2 pounds of beef stew meat
2 tablespoons flour
3 tablespoons olive oil (light, regular or extra-virgin all work)
1 teaspoon salt
½ teaspoon black pepper
6 small potatoes, diced
6 medium carrots, chunked
4 large onions, quartered
¼ cup soy sauce
1 cup water
1 - 10 ¾ ounce can cream of mushroom soup
2 tablespoons lemon juice
1 - 8 ounce package refrigerated biscuits

Roll meat in flour. Heat oil in a deep pot or a Dutch oven then add meat and brown, stirring constantly. Add potatoes, carrots, onions, soy sauce and water. Cover and simmer one hour. Add soup and lemon juice. Arrange the biscuits on top and bake uncovered in a 400° oven for 10 minutes or till the biscuits are browned.

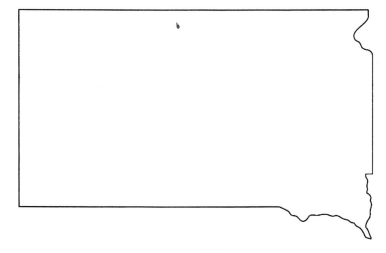

My Husband's Easy Enchiladas

Fast, easy and good! After I made it the first time, my husband gave me the ultimate compliment; he told me it was just like his mom used to make for him growing up.

Flour tortillas, as many as you want
Prepared enchilada sauce, as much as you want
Meat of your choice, as much as you want
Salsa, as much as you want
Sour cream, as much as you want
Pickled chopped jalapeno peppers, as much as you want
Chopped garlic, as much as you want
Chopped onion, as much as you want
Shredded cheese, any kind and as much as you want

Dip tortillas in warmed enchilada sauce. Fill each tortilla with meat, salsa, sour cream, jalapenos, garlic, onion and cheese. Place enchilada's seam down in your baking dish and pour enchilada sauce over the top then add more cheese. Bake at 350° for 35 minutes then turn oven up to 375° and bake for 10 minutes longer.

Food Fact:
The first practical can opener was developed over 40 years after the birth of the metal can. Canned food was invented for the British Navy in 1813 but to open the can they had to use a chisel and hammer. The first can opener was patented in 1858 but the grocery store clerk had to open each can before it could be taken home.

Hearty Beef Gravy on Toast

A frequent comfort food request from my husband and it only takes minutes to make. Best served on top of buttered toast, hot biscuits or mashed potatoes.

1 pound ground beef or sausage
3 tablespoons flour
2 cups milk
1 - 10 ¾ ounce can cream of mushroom soup
Salt to taste

Cook burger or sausage and drain fat if needed. Mix in flour and cook for one minute. Add milk and stir. Cook until it thickens then add soup and heat through. You could also use vegetarian crumbles in place of the meat.

State Fair Grinders

Inspired when we went to the Iowa State Fair one year where my husband had his first Grinder. They can be made ahead and heated just before serving. If you do that and they are cold, they will need 10 minutes longer in the oven.

1 tablespoon olive oil (light, regular or extra-virgin all work)
Either 1 pound sausage (for meat eaters) *or* 2 medium zucchini, small dice (for vegetarians)
1 cup marinara sauce
1 small onion, sliced
Sliced cheese (Gruyere, Velveeta, Provolone and pepper jack are best)
¼ teaspoon anise seed
Big pinch red pepper flakes
Pinch of salt
Black pepper to taste
4 – 6-inch sandwich rolls, split

Preheat oven to 350°. Add oil to a skillet over medium heat and add either sausage or zucchini (depending on which you choose). Add onion and cook for 10 minutes. Add red pepper flakes, anise, salt and pepper then stir in the marinara and heat through. Toast the rolls lightly then line each side with cheese. Spoon a generous amount of the zucchini or sausage mixture onto each roll. Close the rolls and wrap individually in foil. Bake for 15 minutes.

My Mom's Lasagna

My mom's signature dish and her secret ingredient is anise. This will become your new favorite. This is what my mom made for dinner for my husband the first time she and my dad ever met him.

2 pounds sweet Italian sausage
1 tablespoon dried basil
½ to 1 teaspoon salt (taste first before you add a full teaspoon)
2 teaspoons anise seed
2 - 14 ounce cans diced tomatoes
1 - 12 ounce can tomato paste
10 ounces uncooked lasagna noodles (you don't need special noodles, regular ones work perfectly)
3 cups ricotta cheese
½ cup Parmesan cheese, shredded
1 handful parsley, chopped
2 eggs, beaten
½ teaspoon black pepper
1 pound mozzarella cheese, sliced thin

Brown sausage, then add basil, salt, anise seed, diced tomatoes and tomato paste. Simmer uncovered for 30 minutes, stirring occasionally. Combine ricotta, Parmesan, parsley, eggs and pepper and set aside. Use either two large bread loaf pans or one 9x13-inch pan. Layer evenly in this order: sauce, uncooked noodles, ricotta mixture, mozzarella and sauce. Repeat. You will end up with three layers of sauce, two layers of uncooked noodles, two of ricotta mixture and two layers of mozzarella in case that helps you k track. Bake in a preheated 350° oven for 90 minutes. Check it at an hour to make sure meat sauce is not burning. If you make this ahead and cook it cold from the refrigerator, you'll need to bake it for two hours.

Barb's Tetrazzini

We had this often growing up and it was always a hit with left-over Thanksgiving turkey. If it makes more sauce then you like, use the extra on your next pizza, or add some cheese to it and toss it with cooked noodles. As the Tetrazzini sits over night in the fridge, it tends to soak up the sauce.

¾ cup butter
½ cup plus 2 tablespoons flour
5 cups of broth (vegetable or chicken)
2 ½ cups half-and-half
1 ½ cups dry white wine
1 ½ cups Parmesan cheese, shredded
1 pound mushrooms (or even more if you like), sliced
8 ounces uncooked noodles (spaghetti or wide egg are best)
3 – 4 cups cooked chicken or turkey, sliced in bite sized pieces.
Salt and black pepper to taste

To a large saucepan, melt four tablespoons of the butter, add the flour and cook for a minute. Gradually add the broth, wine and half-and-half. Whisk together well and cook, stirring for three minutes. Stir in ¾ cup Parmesan. Then take out 2 ½ cups of the sauce and set aside. In another pan, melt the remaining butter, add mushrooms and cook till softened. When cooked, reserve a cup and set aside. Bring a large pot of water to a boil, add noodles, put a lid on the pan and turn the heat off. Let it sit on the burner that has now been turned off for 20 minutes Drain. Add the noodles, mushrooms and meat to the sauce, toss well to coat. Turn into a shallow baking pan, pour reserved sauce on top of the noodles, add reserved mushrooms and bake for 15 minutes at 375°. Then turn on the broiler and broil it until the tops gets nice and caramelized. Make sure you watch it so it doesn't burn.

```
Food Fact:
With two forks and a charge, a pickle will emit light.
It will actually glow red.
```

Texas Tailgate Beans and Rice

This is a recipe I made up after my husband requested it one night. It can be served over rice or buttered toast.

1 cup long-grain white rice
2 cups water
1 teaspoon chili powder
½ teaspoon ground cumin
½ teaspoon cayenne pepper
2 tablespoons butter
1 onion, chopped
½ red pepper, chopped
12 ounces smoked cooked sausage, thinly sliced
2 - 15 ounce cans kidney beans, drained
1 - 14.5 ounce can diced tomatoes and juice

Bring the rice and water to boil in a pot. Cover, reduce heat to low and simmer 20 minutes. In a skillet, melt butter over medium heat. Add sausage, onion and pepper and cook for 5 minutes. Add beans and tomatoes and continue cooking until heated through. Serve over rice or buttered toast.

Spicy Chocolate Coffee Chili

I know it sounds weird, coffee and chocolate in chili, but my sister Lynn always has people ask her for this recipe. It will become one of your favorites! My husband likes it best without the brown sugar.

2 tablespoons olive oil (light, regular or extra-virgin all work)
2 onions, chopped
3 cloves garlic, minced
1 pound ground beef
¾ pound beef sirloin, cubed
1 - 14.5 ounce can peeled and diced tomatoes with juice
4 - 15 ounce cans pinto beans
12 ounces dark beer
1 cup strong brewed coffee
2 - 6 ounce cans tomato paste
1 - 14 ounce can beef broth
½ cup brown sugar, firmly packed
3 ½ tablespoons chili powder
2 jalapeno peppers, seeded and chopped
1 tablespoon cumin seeds
1 tablespoon unsweetened cocoa powder
1 teaspoon dried oregano
1 teaspoon ground cayenne pepper
1 teaspoon ground coriander
1 teaspoon salt

Heat oil in a large saucepan over medium heat. Cook onions, garlic, ground beef and sirloin in oil for 10 minutes, or until the meat is well browned and the onions are tender. Mix in the diced tomatoes with juice, beer, coffee, tomato paste and beef broth. Season with brown sugar, chili powder, cumin, cocoa powder, oregano, cayenne pepper, coriander and salt. Stir in two cans of the beans and jalapeno peppers. Reduce heat to low, simmer for 1 ½ hours. Stir in the two remaining cans of beans, simmer for 30 minutes then serve. Garnish with shredded cheese if desired.

Seattle Salmon Burgers

Big lemon flavor! Great with horseradish, dill pickles or relish. These freeze well too.

1 - 6 ounce can salmon, rinsed and drained
1 egg
2 tablespoons parsley, chopped
2 tablespoons onion, finely chopped
¼ cup bread crumbs (or cornflake crumbs)
Juice and zest of one lemon (zest the lemons before you juice them)
1 tablespoon capers, rough chopped
½ teaspoon dried basil
Pinch of red pepper flakes

Sauce:
3 tablespoons mayonnaise
1 tablespoon lemon juice
1 pinch dried dill weed
Hot sauce to taste

Mix everything together except the sauce ingredients, shape into two or three patties. Bake at 400° for 20 minutes on a sheet sprayed with cooking spray. When serving, top each patty with sauce.

Pucker Up Cod

This is very, very, very tangy and very, very, very delicious!

4 pieces of cod, (any other white fish will also do)
½ cup flour
3 tablespoons butter
1 teaspoon lemon zest (zest the lemon before you juice it)
2 tablespoons lemon juice
1 tablespoon capers, chopped
1 teaspoon salt
1 teaspoon black pepper

Combine flour, salt and pepper in a shallow plate. Rinse fish well then pat dry. Heat butter in a large pan and brown it. Dredge fillets in seasoned flour on both sides and place in pan. Cook two minutes. Turn carefully and cook two minutes on the other side. Add capers, zest and lemon juice. Arrange fish on serving plate and pour all of the pan drippings on top as well. Wonderful served with a crusty loaf of sourdough bread.

Food Fact:
The spotted climbing perch is able to absorb oxygen from the air and will crawl over land using its strong pectoral fins.

Nutty Coconut Fish

Hands down, my husband's favorite way to eat fish. It is a regular at our home and even 'I don't like fish" people love it and ask for the recipe. If you rinse your fish in cold water before using it, the fishy taste gets washed away.

1 pound white fish fillets, rinsed well then patted dry (we prefer to use cod)
¼ cup mayonnaise
½ cup spicy brown mustard
1 cup bread crumbs
2 cups sweetened, flaked coconut
2 cups salted cashews, chopped (any salted nut will do)
¼ cup white sugar
1 teaspoon salt
½ teaspoon cayenne pepper

Preheat oven to 400°. Lightly grease a cookie sheet. In a small bowl, ble mayonnaise and mustard and set aside. In another bowl, mix coconut, crumbs, nuts, sugar, salt and cayenne pepper. Coat one side of the fish with the mayonnaise mixture then lay it on the coconut mixture and press well. Pick it up and turn it over. Coat the other side of the fish with the mayonnaise mixture, then sprinkle the coconut mixture into that side and press it into the fish, coating well. Put fish on the cookie sheet and bake 20 minutes.

Unforgettable Fish

My sister Lynn said this was good and she was right! Creamy, delicate and yummy!

2 pounds white fish fillets, rinsed well, then patted dry
½ cup Parmesan cheese, grated
¼ cup butter, softened
3 tablespoons mayonnaise
2 tablespoons lemon juice
¼ teaspoon dried basil
¼ teaspoon black pepper
⅛ teaspoon onion powder
⅛ teaspoon celery seed
Salt to taste

Preheat broiler. Line a pan with foil then coat the foil with cooking spray. Mix the Parmesan, butter, mayonnaise, lemon juice, basil, pepper, onion powder and celery salt. Arrange fish in a single layer, sprinkle with salt and broil a few inches from the heat 2-3 minutes. Flip, sprinkle with salt and broil three minutes longer. Remove and cover top with Parmesan mixture and broil two minutes or until it is browned. Spoon any sauce that fell off in the pan over the fish then serve.

```
Food Fact:
England discovered the fork in 1608 but they were not sure
  about them as they considered forks more as jewelry.
 In America, the fork was not widely used until the 18th
                        century.
```

Miso Happy Salmon

My mom's specialty. Everyone will ask how you made it. Try it on cod, halibut, tuna or mahi mahi too.

¼ cup brown sugar, firmly packed
2 tablespoons soy sauce
2 tablespoons hot water
2 tablespoons miso paste (any color is fine)
4 - 6 ounce salmon filets
2 tablespoons chives, chopped
2 lemons
White sugar

Preheat broiler. Whisk together brown sugar, soy sauce, hot water and miso paste. Arrange fish in a shallow baking dish coated with cooking spray. Spoon miso mixture evenly over fish. Broil for 10 minutes, basting twice with miso mixture. While that grills, cut lemons in half. Dip each half in sugar to coat it. Place sugar side down on a grill pan and grill lemons until sugar turns dark and you can see grill marks. Garnish each piece of salmon with a half a sugared lemon and a sprinkle of chives.

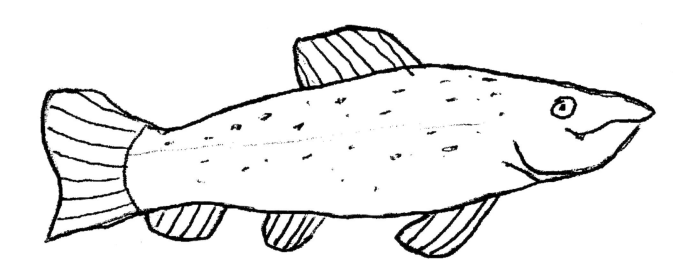

Tongue Tantalizing Tuna Burgers

This is better than a cold tuna fish sandwich any day! I make extra and freeze the patties.

1 - 5 ounce can tuna, drained
1 egg
½ cup bread crumbs
⅓ cup onion, minced
¼ cup celery, minced
¼ - ½ cup mayonnaise
2 tablespoons prepared chili sauce
½ teaspoon dried dill
¼ teaspoon salt
¼ teaspoon black pepper
Hot pepper sauce to taste
Dash Worcestershire sauce

Preheat oven to 400°. Mix everything together, shape into three or four patties and bake for 20 minutes on a cookie sheet that has been sprayed with cooking spray.

Tasty Halibut Steak

This tender fish is the perfect light summer meal. It also works well with cod.

4 halibut steaks, rinsed and patted dry
½ cup sour cream
½ cup mayonnaise
¼ cup Parmesan cheese, grated
4 tablespoons green onion tops, sliced thin
2 tablespoons parsley, chopped
½ teaspoon each: onion powder, dried dill and dry mustard
Salt and black pepper to taste

Place fish in a shallow buttered dish. Blend remaining ingredients and evenly spread on top of fish. Bake at 400° for 20 minutes.

Tuna Noodle Comfort Casserole

Just like what mom made for us growing up. Its comfort food from your childhood.

1 - 10 ¾ ounce cream of celery soup
1 - 10 ¾ ounce can cream of mushroom soup
½ cup milk
2 ½ cups frozen peas
2 tablespoons pimentos, chopped
1 small onion, chopped
5—5 ounce cans tuna, drained
4 cups cooked egg noodles
1 teaspoon Worcestershire sauce
6 tablespoons bread crumbs or crushed potato chips
3 tablespoons butter, melted
Black pepper to taste

Preheat oven to 400°. Mix soups, milk, peas, pimiento, onion, tuna and noodles in 1 ½ quart baking dish. Bake for 30 minutes. Mix crumbs or potato chips with butter then sprinkle that on top of the tuna mixture and bake 5 minutes longer.

7

MEATLESS MAIN DISHES

Magnificent Mac and Cheese

This turned out to be the No. 1 mac and cheese recipe when 10 of my friends and I got together to find the quintessential mac and cheese. It is perfection! Kids love it too!

1 pound uncooked elbow macaroni
2 pounds Velveeta cheese, cut in cubes
1 - 12 ounce can evaporated milk
2 eggs, slightly beaten
½ cup butter, melted
1 cup milk
Black pepper to taste

Spray your crock pot with cooking spray and set aside. Cook macaroni for three minutes in boiling water then remove from water and add to crock pot along with cheese, evaporated milk, eggs, butter, milk and pepper to taste. Cook on low for three hours, stirring once.

No Moo Mac and Cheese

I know using raw cashews to create a cheese sauce sounds odd, but try it! This is so good that I can eat the entire pan. This makes a lot of sauce but it will soak into the pasta as it bakes.

8 ounces uncooked elbow macaroni
⅓ cup plus 1 tablespoon olive oil (light, regular or extra-virgin all work)
1 medium onion, chopped
1 cup raw cashews
⅓ cup lemon juice
1 ⅓ cups water
1 teaspoon salt
1 teaspoon onion powder
1 cup nutritional yeast flakes (purchased at health food stores)

Preheat oven to 375°. Bring a large pot of water to a boil, add the noodles, put a lid on the pan and turn the heat off. Let it sit on the burner that has now been turned off for 20 minutes. Then drain and place pasta in a shallow baking dish. Sauté onion in one tablespoon oil, cook until tender then mix with pasta. In a blender, add cashews, lemon juice, water, salt, ⅓ cup olive oil, yeast and onion powder and process until smooth. Pour that over the pasta and bake for 30 minutes.

Food Fact:
In 1850, Joel Houghton patented a wooden machine with a hand turned wheel that splashed water on dishes. It was hardly workable but it received the first ever dishwasher patent.

Miss Grunion's Gooey Gomito

The gooey-est, yummy-est, cheesy-est meal you will ever eat! A lot of ingredients but well worth it. It freezes wonderfully and it also keeps for days in the refrigerator.

1 pound uncooked gomito, penne, radiatore or cavatappi pasta

1 - 15 ounce can diced tomatoes

1 - 6 ounce can tomato paste

1 - 10 ounce can spicy Rotel tomatoes

1 medium onion, chopped

1 ½ pounds mushrooms, quartered

¼ cup green olives, sliced

4 green onions, sliced

¼ cup parsley, chopped

1 ½ teaspoons anise seed

2 tablespoons capers, chopped

1 tablespoon dried basil

1 teaspoon red pepper flakes

2 - 4 ½ ounce cans sliced black olives, rinsed and drained

6 ounces Cheddar cheese, shredded

6 ounces Monterey Jack cheese, shredded

8 ounces Velveeta cheese, sliced

8 ounces cream cheese, cubed

Salt to taste

In a large pot add diced tomatoes, tomato paste, Rotel, chopped onion, black olives, mushrooms, anise seed, capers, basil, red pepper flakes, green olives, parsley and salt. Cook on medium low for 30 minutes, stirring occasionally. Turn oven on to 375°. As the sauce is cooking, place pasta in large pot of boiling water for 5 minutes then drain and set aside. Use large oven proof deep baking dish (I use a soup pot), put in a layer of half the sauce, then a layer of half the pasta, then a layer of half of all three cheeses plus a layer of the cream cheese. Repeat layers one more time then top with the green onions and bake covered for one hour.

Parmesan Pasta Florentine

My aunt Jean's been making this for years. I made it my own by adding more cheese, lemon juice and butter.

1 pound uncooked ziti pasta (penne, radiatore or cavatappi also works)
½ cup butter
3 tablespoons lemon juice
5 ounces Gorgonzola cheese, crumbled
1 bag pre-washed spinach
½ cup Parmesan cheese, shredded
Salt and pepper to taste

Bring a large pot of water to a boil, add the noodles, put a lid on the pan and turn the heat off. Let it sit on the burner that has now been turned off for 20 minutes. Drain, then set aside. Melt butter in large skillet. Add lemon juice, Gorgonzola, ¼ cup of Parmesan and stir until cheese is melted. Season with salt and pepper. Add pasta and spinach to the cheese mixture and toss well. To serve, top with the remaining Parmesan.

```
                         Food Fact:
    The first American pasta factory was opened in Brooklyn,
  New York in 1848. A horse was kept in the basement to power
  the machinery. To dry the spaghetti, strands were placed on
                   the roof to dry in the sunshine.
```

Fork-A-Roni and Cheese

This was the No. 2 mac and cheese recipe out of 10 at a party I had while writing this book. It was only No. 2 because it is mildly spicy and kids might not like it as well.

16 ounces uncooked elbow macaroni
½ cups butter
¼ cups flour
2 cups milk
½ pound sharp Cheddar cheese, in small cubes
½ pound pepper jack cheese, in small cubes
½ pound Velveeta cheese, in small cubes

Bring a large pot of water to a boil, add the macaroni, put a lid on the pan and turn the heat off. Let it sit on the burner that has now been turned off for 20 minutes. Melt butter on medium heat then add flour and cook one minute, whisking frequently. Add milk and whisk till smooth. Let it thicken for a few minutes then add all the cheese and whisk till melted. Pour immediately over hot, drained pasta.

Curry Pocket Sandwiches

Do not miss out on these, even if you're not sure you like curry because it is just a hint of that curry taste. These are great for picnics and the ball park as they travel so well and aren't messy to eat on the go.

1 - 8 ounce package crescent rolls (I often use the crescent roll full sheets).
1 tablespoon olive oil (light, regular or extra-virgin all work)
¼ cup onion, very small dice
½ cup potatoes, very small dice
½ cup carrots, very small dice
½ cup frozen peas
2 ½ teaspoons soy sauce
¼ teaspoon curry powder
¼ teaspoon ground cumin
¼ teaspoon ground coriander
¼ teaspoon ground ginger
¼ teaspoon turmeric
Pinch of salt and red pepper flakes

Preheat oven to 375°. Place diced carrots and potatoes in a pan of water, bring to a boil and cook until tender. Drain and place potatoes and carrots in frying pan with oil, onion and frozen peas and sauté for three minutes. Add soy sauce, curry, cumin, coriander, ginger, turmeric, salt and red pepper flakes and cook for two minutes. If you use regular size crescent rolls: Separate rolls into four short rectangles and press the seams together. Cut each rectangle in half to make squares. Spoon a big mound of filling on top of one square then place another square on top of that and do your best to seal it closed. If you use large size crescent rolls, separate rolls into 6 triangles. Spoon a big mound of filling on top of each. Fold dough over to cover all the filling and pinch edges together. Bake on sheets sprayed with cooking spray for 15-18 minutes. *The possibilities for fillings for these are endless – maybe shredded beef, cheese, sour cream and hot peppers or maybe corned beef, sauerkraut and thousand island dressing; pizza toppers and marinara work great too. These can be made in advance and baked later. If cold, let them get to room temperature or they will need to be baked longer.

Sour Cream Mushroom Stroganoff

My mom always made this when we were growing up and it is still a favorite today. It is the best stroganoff I have ever tasted; rich and thick and amazing! This is my mom's original recipe but I also tell in parenthesis how I make it.

16 ounces uncooked egg noodles
2 tablespoons butter (I use 4 tablespoons)
1 large onion, chopped (I use 2)
1 pound mushrooms, chopped (I use 2 pounds)
7 ounces beef or vegetable broth (I use 14 ounces)
1 tablespoon Worcestershire sauce (I use 2 tablespoons)
1 tablespoon lemon juice (I use 2 tablespoons)
1 tablespoon ketchup (I use 2 tablespoons)
3 tablespoons flour (I use 6 tablespoons)
Chopped parsley to taste (I use ¼ cup)
Sour cream to taste (I use at least 1 ½ cups)
Salt and black pepper to taste
1 pound round steak, in bite size pieces (optional)

Sauté onion in butter until tender, then add the mushrooms and cook for 5 minutes. If you are using steak, add it now and sauté it for 5 more minutes. Push the vegetables and meat (if using) to the sides of the pan to create a space in the middle and whisk the flour and broth together, cooking for three minutes, whisking constantly. Then add the ketchup, lemon juice and Worcestershire. Mix well and cook on medium until the sauce has thickened. As that thickens, bring a large pot of water to a boil, then add the noodles, put a lid on the pan and turn the heat off. Let it sit on the burner that has now been turned off for 20 minutes. Then drain and toss with parsley. When the sauce has gotten as think as you want it, turn the heat to low and add sour cream and salt and pepper to taste. Do not let it boil once the sour cream is added. To serve, pour the mushroom sauce over the noodles or serve the noodles separately from the sauce.

Salsa Bean Burgers

The bean burgers are packed with flavor and healthy and good for you too.

1 carrot, finely chopped
1 - 15 ounce can kidney beans, rinsed and drained
1 tablespoon olive oil (light, regular or extra-virgin all work)
½ cup onion, chopped
¾ cup prepared salsa
¼ cup cilantro, chopped
½ cup rolled oats (quick or old-fashioned)
½ cup cooked brown rice
½ teaspoon black pepper
Salt to taste
Chili powder to taste (I use a big pinch)
Ground cumin to taste (I use a big pinch)

Preheat oven to 425°. Put oil in frying pan, add onion and carrot and cook till tender. In a large bowl, combine the onion mixture, salsa, cilantro, rolled oats, rice, pepper, salt, chili powder and cumin. Form into patties and place on baking sheet sprayed with cooking spray and cook for 15 minutes.

Chow Train Vegetarian Chili

This takes minutes to make and its even better the next day. I sometimes add a bit of prepared barbeque sauce for a richer, sweeter chili.

½ large onion, chopped
2 jalapeno peppers, finely chopped
1 - 28 ounce can diced tomatoes with juice
1 - 4 ounce can green chilies, chopped
1 - 15.5 ounce can kidney beans, rinsed
1 - 15.5 ounce can pinto beans, rinsed
1 - 15.5 ounce can black beans, rinsed
1 - 14.5 ounce can creamed corn
1 - 6 ounce can tomato paste
1 - 12 ounce can low sodium V8 juice
¼ cup soy sauce
1 tablespoon black pepper
2 tablespoons dried oregano
2 teaspoons ground cumin
⅓ cup chili powder (I know it sounds like a lot but it is not!)
¼ cup ketchup

Combine everything in a slow cooker; cook on low 6-8 hours or high for four hours.

Indescribably Good 'Raw' Lasagna

You can make this without a dehydrator; just warm it in the oven on the lowest heat.
It takes a bit of time but it is worth it! You won't believe how creamy it is.

Sauce:
16 ounces sun-dried tomatoes, packed in oil
7 Roma tomatoes
½ teaspoon salt
1 tablespoon onion, chopped
2 tablespoons lemon juice
2 teaspoons dried basil
1 teaspoon dried oregano
½ teaspoon dried thyme
1 tablespoon honey
Red pepper flakes to taste
Blend everything together in a blender or processor until smooth then set aside.

Mushroom Layer:
4 cups sliced mushrooms
3 tablespoons soy sauce
1 tablespoon miso paste
2 tablespoons water
2 tablespoons olive oil (light, regular or extra-virgin all work
Combine all and let marinate for two hours. Drain and set aside.

Onion/Pepper Layer:
1 small onion, sliced thin
2 red bell peppers, sliced thin
2 tablespoons olive oil (light, regular or extra-virgin all work)
2 tablespoons lemon juice
Pinch of salt
Combine all and let marinate for two hours. Drain and set aside.

'Cheese Sauce:'
1 cup raw cashews
½ cup macadamia nuts
2 tablespoons pine nuts
½ teaspoon salt
2 tablespoons lemon juice
1 tablespoon parsley, chopped
1 cup water
Blend everything together in a blender or processor until smooth then set aside.

You will also need:
Three or four zucchini, sliced lengthwise as thinly as you can (to create 'noodles')
1 layer of spinach leaves
1 cup Kalamata olives, drained and chopped

Assembly: To help you keep track—you'll need zucchini three times, spinach once and all else twice. Put slices of zucchini on bottom of 9x13-inch pan. Then layer in this order; 'cheese' sauce, mushrooms, zucchini, tomato sauce, onions/peppers, zucchini, cheese sauce, spinach, mushrooms, onions/peppers, tomato sauce and end up with olives evenly sprinkled over top. Cover with plastic wrap & put in the fridge for four hours. Remove plastic wrap and put in a dehydrator at 135° for four hours or in a regular oven on the lowest setting you have.

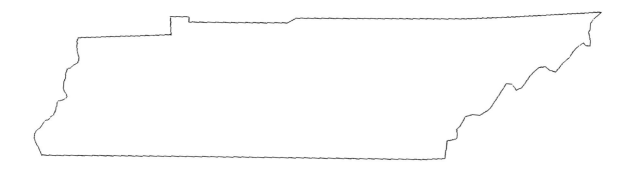

Nashville Dilled Cheese Sandwich

Gruyere cheese has a nutty, mild taste and it is the best melting cheese. If I had known about Gruyere years ago I'd have had a lifetime of amazing grilled cheese sandwiches.

Sliced bread, any kind you like
Sliced Gruyere cheese, as much as you want
Sliced red onion, as much as you want
Sliced dill pickles, as much as you want
Mayonnaise, as much as you want
Butter, as much as you want

Lay two pieces of bread flat. Spread mayonnaise on both. Cover that with cheese. On top of that add onion and pickles then place the other piece of bread on top. Melt butter in a pan. Place sandwich in that pan and put some weight on top of it - either another heavy pan or a cookie sheet that has something heavy on it. The sandwich will cook quicker if it is weighted but you need to check it often to make sure it is not burning. Flip it over when it is golden brown. Check it often once you flip it and remove it from the pan when it is toasty and golden brown.

Delicious Portobello Sandwich

Even meat eaters will like these. Don't leave out the capers though, they make it!

6 tablespoons olive oil (light, regular or extra-virgin all work)
½ teaspoon dried thyme
2 tablespoons balsamic vinegar
4 large Portobello mushrooms
4 extra large buns
¼ cup mayonnaise
1 heaping tablespoon capers, drained and chopped
Salt and black pepper to taste

In a mixing bowl, make the dressing by combining oil, thyme, vinegar, salt and pepper. Put the mushroom caps, bottom side up, in a shallow baking pan. Brush the caps with ½ the dressing. Put them under the broiler and cook for 5 minutes. Flip the mushrooms and brush with the remaining dressing and broil four minutes longer. In a small bowl, mix capers and mayonnaise then spread that on lightly toasted buns, add the mushrooms and enjoy!

Food Fact:
The potato was the first food ever to be grown in outer space. Astronauts took potato plants on the space shuttle Columbia in 1995 to see if they could grow them in zero gravity. The experiment was a success.

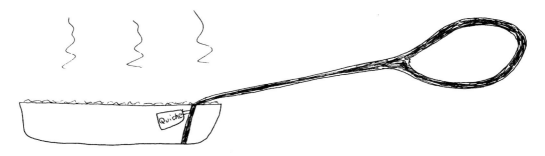

Quiche On A Leash

This is a favorite of my husband. For the crust, I use a half recipe of my Perfect Pie Crust but I omit the sugar. I use a deep dish pie plate to make sure no liquid bubbles over. The quiche also makes a great filling for my Homemade Flour Tortilla's.

6 large eggs
1 tablespoon butter
1 yellow or red pepper, seeded and chopped
1 – 6.5 ounce can mushrooms, rinsed and drained (can use 6 ounces fresh mushrooms but you must drain onion/mushroom mixture before placing in pie shell)
1 – 4 ounce can chopped green chilies, drained
1 small onion, chopped
8 ounces of shredded cheese, any kind you like
½ cup liquid non dairy creamer
½ cup water
⅛ teaspoon cayenne pepper
1 – 9-inch pie shell, unbaked
Salt to taste (I salt after it is baked as the cheese adds a lot of sodium)

Add butter to a large skillet and sauté the peppers and onion until they just start to get soft. Then add the mushrooms and chilies, stir then remove from heat. If you use fresh mushrooms, cook until they are softened. In a bowl, combine the eggs, creamer, water and cayenne. Spoon the pepper/onion mix evenly into pie shell. Sprinkle four ounces of cheese on top and pour egg mix evenly over all. Top with remaining four ounces of cheese, place pie plate on a sheet pan and bake at 375° for 55 minutes. It will be puffed up when done but it will deflate as it cools. Let rest for 10 minutes before serving.

Cowboy Spaghetti Pie

This just hits the spot for me. It is excellent for breakfast, lunch or dinner and its good cold too.

8 ounces uncooked spaghetti noodles
5 tablespoons olive oil (light, regular or extra-virgin all work)
¼ pound mushrooms, chopped
1 medium onion, minced
½ cup Parmesan cheese, shredded or grated
10 large eggs, lightly beaten
½ cup heavy cream or half-and-half
¼ cup butter
Small handful fresh parsley, chopped
1 teaspoon salt
½ teaspoon black pepper
Pinch red pepper flakes

Preheat oven to 425°. Bring a large pot of water to a boil, add the spaghetti, put a lid on the pan and turn the heat off. Let it sit on the burner that has now been turned off for 20 minutes. Then rinse, drain and set aside. In a large oven proof skillet over medium, sauté the onion and mushroom in olive oil. Add butter and cream or half-and-half and cook for three minutes. Add Parmesan, cooked noodles, salt, pepper, parsley and eggs and mix together well. Stir it constantly as the eggs set, then smooth the top to make it flat and put it in the oven to bake for 10 minutes. *For a variation, before you bake it, you can add a few handfuls of cooked meat in with the egg mixture.

8

VEGETABLE SIDES, SAUCES AND MORE

Back in the Saddle Spuds

These are crisp on the outside but so tender on the inside.

4 baking potatoes, skins on (or 5 smaller potatoes like Yukon Gold)
4 tablespoons butter, melted
Salt and black pepper to taste
4 tablespoons Parmesan cheese, grated
1 tablespoon seasoned bread crumbs

Preheat oven to 425°. Place potatoes on a flat surface and place the handle of a wooden spoon on one side, right next to the potato. Make slices across the potato the short way; ⅛ to ¼ inches apart, cutting down to the handle. This will stop the potatoes from being cut all the way through as the slices must stay connected at the bottom. Place potatoes, cut side up in a shallow baking dish and drizzle with half the butter, then season with salt and pepper. Bake 35 minutes then remove from the oven, drizzle with the remaining butter and sprinkle with Parmesan and bread crumbs and return to the oven for 20 minutes longer. *Can use olive oil for butter and you can add garlic powder too.

Cheesy Scalloped Potatoes

This is my mom's recipe that we grew up on and we always had it Christmas Day with ham and guacamole as a side dish. I leave the skins on the potatoes as well.

Potatoes, any kind, cut in ¼-inch slices and enough to fill a 9x13-inch pan
3 tablespoons butter
3 tablespoons flour
3 ½ cups milk (I often use oat milk for the extra flavor it gives)
4 ounces Cheddar cheese, shredded
5 ounces Velveeta cheese, cubed
1 teaspoon salt
1 teaspoon pepper

In a small saucepan over medium heat, melt butter. Add flour and whisk for two minutes. Pour in milk, stirring occasionally as it thickens. After about 5 minutes, add cheeses and stir until melted. Add salt and pepper. Fill half the pan with potatoes; evenly distributed, then pour ½ the cheese sauce over them. Evenly layer the rest of the potatoes on top of that and the remaining cheese sauce. Bake at 350° for 1 ½ hours.

Ranch Mashers

These are full of flavor and so easy to make. They easily double or triple as well!

6 large potatoes, quartered
4 ounces cream cheese, softened
¼ cup butter, softened
¼ cup milk
2 - 1.4 ounce packages dry ranch salad dressing mix
1 heaping teaspoon dried parsley

Cover potatoes with water in a pan. Bring to a boil and cook until tender. Drain and mash them with cream cheese, butter, ranch dressing mix and parsley. Add that to slow cooker, cover and cook on low for three hours.

Potato Crisps with Pink Sauce

Better than French fries and dipped in the pink sauce, they're hard to stop eating!

Any kind of potato you like and as many as you want
Olive oil (light, regular or extra-virgin all work)
Salt and black pepper to taste
½ cup mayonnaise
½ cup store bought barbeque sauce

Place a large cookie sheet in the oven, then turn the temperature to 450°. Slice the potatoes in ¼-inch slices. Toss them in enough oil to coat them well then season with salt and pepper. Carefully place potatoes on the hot cookie sheet in a single layer. It may smoke when you add them and that is normal. Cook for 20 minutes. Flip over with a metal spatula and cook 5-15 minutes longer (depending on how crispy you like them.)

Pink Sauce:
Mix mayonnaise and barbeque sauce together. Serve with the crisps.

Rich Scalloped Potatoes

Two words: Simply amazing!

¾ cup extra sharp Cheddar cheese, shredded and firmly packed

¾ cup Gorgonzola cheese, crumbled

⅓ cup Parmesan cheese, shredded and firmly packed

4 pounds Yukon Gold potatoes, peeled, cut into ¼ -inch thick rounds

1 ½ teaspoons salt

½ teaspoon black pepper

¼ cup onion, finely chopped

3 tablespoons flour

4 tablespoons butter

3 cups whole milk

Preheat oven to 400°. Lightly butter a 9x13-inch baking dish. Mix the three cheeses in a small bowl and set aside. Arrange half the potatoes in a baking dish, slightly overlapping. Sprinkle with one teaspoon salt and ¼ teaspoon pepper. Add onion over that then the flour. Dot with two tablespoons butter. Sprinkle half of the cheese mixture over top. Add the remaining potatoes, ½ teaspoon salt, ¼ teaspoon pepper and two tablespoons butter. Reserve remaining cheese. Bring milk to simmer in pan. Pour milk over potatoes. Cover baking dish tightly with foil. Bake 45 minutes. Uncover dish; sprinkle potatoes with reserved cheese mixture. Bake uncovered until potatoes are tender and cheese is deep golden brown, about 45 minutes longer. This can be prepared ahead then brought to room temperature and warmed at 375° for 20 minutes. Let stand 15 minutes before serving.

Lemon Feta Wedges

Feta meets lemon juice meets fresh mint meets potatoes…oh yeah, and some butter too.

5 pounds potatoes, any kind you like and cut into wedges
4 cloves garlic, minced
¾ cup olive oil (light, regular or extra-virgin all work)
Zest of one lemon (zest the lemon before you juice it)
½ cup lemon juice, divided
¼ cup butter, melted
1 ½ tablespoons dried oregano
1 tablespoon fresh mint, chopped
16 ounces feta cheese, crumbled
Salt and black pepper to taste

Preheat oven to 450°. Cover a large jelly roll pan with foil then coat with cooking spray. Mix potatoes with oregano, garlic, oil, ¼ cup lemon juice, salt and pepper then pour onto jelly roll pan. Cook 40 minutes uncovered then remove from oven. Mix together the melted butter, lemon zest and the rest of the lemon juice. Pour over the potatoes. Cover loosely with foil and bake 15 minutes longer. Take out, remove foil and sprinkle potatoes with feta and mint and cook 5 minutes more.

Plantain Crisps

So easy and I promise, you won't be able to stop eating them!

2 cups vegetable oil
3 plantains, peeled and cut into 1-inch slices
Salt and garlic powder to taste

Heat the oil in a heavy skillet over medium. Place plantains in and cook for three minutes, then place on paper towels. Put each slice between wax paper and flatten by pushing your palm down on them. Return slices to the skillet and fry until golden, flipping once. Place on paper towels and season with salt and garlic powder.

Honey Cashew Green Beans

The honey, salty nuts and fiery pepper flakes bring these beans alive. It is very good the next day too; either room temperature or right out of the refrigerator.

½ pound green beans, trimmed and cut in bite size pieces
3 tablespoons salted cashews, coarsely chopped (or any salted nut you like)
2 tablespoons butter
1 tablespoon honey
¼ teaspoon salt
Pinch of red pepper flakes

In a medium skillet, cook cashews and green beans in butter for 5 minutes, stirring occasionally. Add honey and salt and cook until the beans are tender.

Ladies On A Bus

These are fabulous and you'll love the tang from the lemon juice. I use nutritional yeast flakes for a change and those on dairy free diets will love them!

3 large Portobello mushrooms
½ onion, minced fine
1 tablespoon butter
2 slices toasted bread, finely diced
1 ½ tablespoons soy sauce
2 tablespoons grated Parmesan cheese or nutritional yeast flakes (at a health food store)
¼ teaspoon dried marjoram
1 lemon
Small handful of fresh parsley

Preheat oven to 350°. Remove mushroom stems and scrape out black gills. Sauté parsley and onion in butter then mix with bread, soy sauce, Parmesan cheese or nutritional yeast flakes and marjoram. Stuff mixture into mushroom tops and sprinkle all three mushrooms equally with the juice of one lemon. Bake for 30 minutes.

Sesame Chili Pasta

I have eaten this for years; it is one of my all-time favorite comfort foods. It must only be made with fresh pasta though.

¼ cup sesame oil

¼ cup soy sauce

2 tablespoons white sugar (can use honey too but you may need a bit less)

2 tablespoons hot chili oil

2 tablespoons black vinegar (from an Asian food store - can also use balsamic vinegar)

1 pound fresh angel hair pasta

½ cup sesame seeds, toasted

1 ½ cups green onions, thinly sliced on the diagonal

In a large bowl, whisk sesame oil, soy sauce, sugar, chili oil and vinegar. Cook pasta in boiling water for one minute. Drain it then immediately toss the pasta in the dressing, completely coating it. Add sesame seeds and half the onions and toss until all the dressing is absorbed. Place pasta on a platter and sprinkle the noodles with the remaining green onions. It is best served at room temperature.

Fuss Free Rice

After years of having mushy rice from my rice cooker, I had to come up with a better way. This is right every time and you don't have to baby-sit it on the stove top.

1 cup uncooked rice, white or brown

6 green onions, sliced

2 tablespoons olive oil (light, regular or extra-virgin all work)

2 cups boiling water (2 ½ cups for brown rice)

Preheat oven to 350°. Put oil in an oven proof pot then add onion and rice and sauté for one minute, stirring constantly. Add boiling water, cover you pan with a lid and bake for 30 minutes (45 minutes for brown rice).

Oven Roasted Sweet Corn

Roasting produces the sweetest corn you will ever taste. You'll never eat it any other way again.

Husk on Corn-on-the-cob, as many as you want
Unsalted butter
Salt
Black pepper

Preheat oven to 350°. Open the end of the corn and trim away the tip if it needs to be. Then remove any silk you can then return the husk back over the corn, covering the corn as best you can. Place the corn directly on the oven rack and roast for 20 minutes. Remove from the oven, peel the husk back and keep it on so you can use to hold the cob instead of corn holders. I use a brush to apply the butter because it goes on much easier. Season with salt and black pepper.

Southern Cornbread Dressing

This is great anytime of year but it is especially good at the holidays.

4 cups cornbread, day old and cut in 1-inch cubes
6 cups sourdough bread, day old and cut in 1-inch cubes
1 cup chopped celery, finely diced
1 cup chopped onion, finely diced
½ cup butter (plus more to butter the baking dish)
2 cups apples, finely diced
2 cups vegetable or chicken broth
½ teaspoon salt
1 teaspoon ground thyme
1 teaspoon ground sage
1 tablespoon poultry seasoning
Black pepper to taste

Allow the diced bread and diced cornbread to sit out overnight to dry. Preheat oven to 350°. In a skillet cook apples, celery and onion in butter until tender. Then add sage, thyme, salt and pepper. Toss this mixture with the sourdough and corn bread. Add broth, a little at a time as you may not need it all. You don't want so much broth that it becomes gummy. Taste it next to see if you want to adjust any seasonings. Pour into a buttered 9x13-inch baking dish and cook for 35 minutes.

```
Food Fact:
The first Thanksgiving feast was held in 1621 and it was
 intended to thank the Lord for sparing the lives of the
survivors of the Mayflower, who had landed at Plymouth Rock
                  on December 11, 1620.
```

Best Fried Green Tomatoes

When I had my first garden I planted 13 tomato plants and got over 100 so this recipe was born.

4 large green tomatoes
2 eggs
½ cup milk
1 cup flour
½ cup cornmeal
½ cup bread crumbs
2 teaspoons salt
¼ teaspoon black pepper
Peanut oil for frying

Slice tomatoes ½-inch thick. Whisk eggs and milk in bowl. Put flour on one plate. On another plate mix cornmeal, bread crumbs, salt and pepper. Dip tomatoes in flour then milk mixture then cornmeal. In skillet, pour in ½-inch of oil, heat over medium and fry 5 tomatoes at a time not letting them touch. When browned, flip, fry on the other side, drain on paper towels, serve with ranch dressing.

Crock Pot Lemon Potatoes

My friend Jordan made these and I knew this had to be the last recipe squeezed in my book.

4 pounds red or Yukon Gold potatoes, peeled and cut in 2-inch cubes
1 cup lemon juice, must be fresh squeezed
½ cup olive oil (light, regular or extra-virgin all work)
4 garlic cloves, minced
1 tablespoon dried oregano
2 tablespoons dried parsley
1 teaspoon salt
½ teaspoon black pepper
1 - 14.5 ounce can of chicken broth (vegetable broth works too)
½ cup Kalamata olive brine

Place the cut potatoes in water while you make the sauce. Combine all ingredients except the potatoes in a blender. Blend for one minute. Pour mixture over potatoes; let sit for two hours in fridge then place in crock pot and cook on high for 5 hours.

Creamy Dijon Brussels Sprouts

These are creamy and wonderful and the only way I'll eat Brussels sprouts now!

2 pounds Brussels sprouts, trimmed and halved
¼ cup olive oil (light, regular or extra-virgin all work)
¼ cup plus 2 tablespoons Dijon mustard
⅔ cup half-and-half or heavy cream
Few pinches of salt
Black pepper to taste

Preheat oven to 375°. Whisk together the half-and half or heavy cream and the mustard then set aside. Place the sprouts on a baking sheet. Drizzle with oil then season with salt and pepper and toss to coat. Roast for 15 minutes then shake the pan, repositioning the sprouts and roast 15 minutes longer. Take the pan out of the oven, pour the cream mixture over top and toss to coat. Return to the oven for 7 minutes. Serve warm or at room temperature.

Pineapple Fried Rice

My husband made a version of this rice when he was a bachelor; then I came along and jazzed it up.

1 cup cooked rice
2 tablespoons olive oil (light, regular or extra-virgin all work)
2 small carrots, grated
1 cup frozen peas
1 - 8 ounce can pineapple rings, drained and rough chopped
3 green onions, sliced
4 eggs
Handful of salted peanuts, chopped
Handful of salted cashews, chopped
Few drops sesame oil
Pinch of red pepper flakes,
Store bought teriyaki sauce, soy sauce and hot sauce to taste

Sauté carrots and green onions in olive oil and after a few minutes add peas and pineapple. Lightly beat four eggs then add to carrot mixture and stir until eggs scrambled. Add peanuts, cashews, rice, sesame oil, pepper flakes, teriyaki sauce, soy sauce and hot sauce. Serve hot.

Coconut Curry Root Vegetables

Just the right amount of spice and just as wonderful days later as the flavors marry. If you wanted to add meat to this dish, that would be easy to do. Just add any cooked meat you like when you toss the vegetables into the pot.

4 cups water
2 cups rice
2 cups sweet onion, cut into half moons
1 tablespoon olive oil (light, regular or extra-virgin all work)
2 tablespoons flour
2 cups vegetable stock
1 acorn squash, peeled, seeds removed, and cut into 1-inch cubes
2 cups broccoli, cut into small florets
2 cups carrot, sliced
1 - 14 oz. can coconut milk
2 cups frozen peas, thawed
3 tablespoons fresh mint, chopped
2 tablespoons curry powder (I usually use more though)
1 teaspoon garlic powder
1 tablespoon honey
½ teaspoon salt
¼ teaspoon black pepper
Red pepper flakes to taste

Place water in a large pan and bring to a boil. Add the rice, cover, reduce heat to low, and simmer for 15 minutes. Remove the pan from the heat, keep the lid on and set aside. In a large pot, cook the onion in oil for 5 minutes. Add the flour, stir well to coat the onions, and cook one minute. Add stock and curry powder and cook over medium heat until slightly thickened. Add the squash, broccoli and carrot, stir well to coat the vegetables. Cover, reduce to low, and simmer for 35 minutes. Add the remaining ingredients, stir and simmer for three minutes. To serve; place rice on large platter and top with the vegetables.

Happy Herb Fries

Kid approved, these taste just like little crispy potato chips!

Fresh basil or sage leaves, as much as you want (onion rings work too)
Olive, coconut, peanut or vegetable oil
Water or lemon-lime soft drink
Flour seasoned with as much as you want of: turmeric, garlic powder, curry powder, onion powder, paprika, salt, pepper and 2 teaspoons of baking powder.

Heat four inches of oil in a heavy bottomed pan on medium-high. While that heats, mix up seasoned flour and add enough water or lemon-lime soft drink to make it the consistency of thick pancake batter. Dip herbs or onions in batter, letting extra batter drip off before adding them to the hot oil. If they stick while cooking, separate apart. Watch as they cook and remove when browned and crispy. If you use soft drink instead of water, they brown a lot faster. Drain on paper towels and sprinkle with salt right away. Keep each batch in a warm oven until finished.

> **Food Fact:**
> During the European Renaissance, fashionable ladies used lemon juice as a way to redden their lips.

Wanna Be Cheese Sauce

This is amazing on steamed broccoli, any vegetable really. I also like to dip potato chips, raw carrots and celery in it. It is also great on rice too!

1 cup raw cashews
⅓ cup lemon juice
1 ⅓ cups water
1 teaspoon salt
⅓ cup olive oil (light, regular or extra-virgin all work)
1 cup nutritional yeast (purchased at health food stores)
1 teaspoon onion powder

Blend until smooth all in a blender or a high speed blender (I like Vitamix or Blendtec) and serve at room temperature.

Smooth as Silk White Sauce

This sauce is the start of many good things; classic chipped beef on toast or you can add shredded cheese and use this on vegetables or pasta. The possibilities are endless.

2 tablespoons butter
2 tablespoons flour
1 cup milk

In a small saucepan over medium heat, melt butter. Add flour and whisk for two minutes. Pour in milk, stirring constantly as it thickens. Add more milk depending on desired consistency. This can easily be doubled or tripled depending on how much you need.

Spicy Peanut Sauce

Good on pasta – cold or hot and it is a great dunker for raw vegetables as well.

1 cup chunky salsa
½ cup chunky peanut butter
2 tablespoons honey
1 heaping tablespoon orange juice concentrate
½ teaspoon ground ginger

...ether peanut butter, honey, concentrate and ginger until smooth.
...salsa and pour into medium pan and heat through, stirring
... Serve over pasta or rice.

Homestead Mushroom Gravy

Our nephew Doug came for dinner and turned this down; but when I told him this gravy was healthy; he tried it and even had seconds.

6 tablespoons flour
6 tablespoons olive oil (light, regular or extra-virgin all work)
3 tablespoons butter
¼ cup onion, diced
¼ cup carrot, diced
¼ cup celery, diced
1 teaspoon dried thyme
1 cup fresh mushrooms, chopped small (can also use 2 – 6.5-ounce cans)
3 cups of vegetable or chicken stock
½ tablespoon soy sauce
½ teaspoon honey

Sauté mushrooms in butter then set aside. Add olive oil and flour to the pan and cook it for 5 minutes, stirring constantly. Add vegetables and spices then lower the heat and let cook three minutes. Stir in the stock then add soy sauce, honey, mushrooms and vegetables. Simmer for 15 minutes to thicken.

Speckled Milk Gravy

This is just right for fried chicken and biscuits. I sometimes use oat milk because I love the flavor it gives this gravy. If gravy is too thin, whisk in potato flakes. They will make the gravy lump free as well.

2 ½ cups milk
3 tablespoons flour
3 tablespoons olive oil (light, regular or extra-virgin all work)
Salt and black pepper to taste

Whisk the flour in oil for three minutes. Whisk in milk and stir frequently until it is thickened, then season to taste.

Pepper Pasta Sauce

For those who have allergies or just don't like tomatoes, this is surprisingly good and if you weren't told it wasn't tomatoes, I am not sure you'd know it.

2 very large red peppers or 3 regular size, seeded and chopped
1 large sweet onion, chopped
Half a zucchini, sliced
2 tablespoons olive oil (light, regular or extra-virgin all work)
2 teaspoons lemon juice
1 teaspoon dried oregano
1 teaspoon dried basil
1 teaspoon ground cumin
1 teaspoon dried thyme
1 teaspoon turmeric
¼ teaspoon salt
Big pinch red pepper flakes
Garlic to taste

Preheat oven to 350°. Place peppers, zucchini and onion on a large pan, toss with olive oil and roast for 45 minutes. Pour vegetables, their juices, seasonings and garlic into a food processor or blender and process until it is as chunky or smooth as you like.

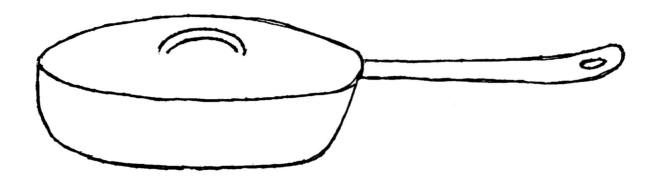

Tomato-Free Spaghetti Sauce

Great for anyone with tomato allergies. It looks, smells and tastes like the real thing! Makes a really good pizza sauce too.

1 onion, finely chopped
1 clove garlic, finely chopped
⅓ cup olive oil (light, regular or extra-virgin all work)
3 tablespoons lemon juice
1 tablespoon balsamic vinegar
1 - 15 ounce can beets, drained (not pickled)
1 - 15 ounce can pumpkin (not pumpkin pie filling)
3 cups water (omit water if you are using this as pizza sauce)
1 tablespoon dried basil
1 tablespoon dried thyme
2 teaspoons dried oregano
1 teaspoon dried marjoram
1 tablespoon honey
1 teaspoon salt
½ teaspoon black pepper
¼ teaspoon red pepper flakes
⅛ teaspoon anise seeds

In a large pot, cook onion and garlic in oil until onion is translucent. As that cooks, puree the beets until smooth and set aside. When the onion is done, add to it lemon juice, vinegar, beets, pumpkin, basil, thyme, oregano, marjoram, honey, red pepper flakes, salt, black pepper and anise seeds. Stir until well combined and cook over low heat for 30-45 minutes to let the herbs soften.

Spicy Chili Pepper BBQ Sauce

For those that cannot have tomatoes, this is zippy and spicy with rich, full flavor.

¾ cup water
3 ounces dried chili peppers, washed, stem removed and seeded
1 cup chopped onion
1 teaspoon cayenne pepper
3 tablespoons apple cider vinegar
3 tablespoons olive oil (light, regular or extra-virgin all work)
1 teaspoon molasses
¼ cup honey
Salt to taste

Simmer all ingredients on the stove for 30 minutes then add to blender and puree. Refrigerate.

9

DESSERT

Perfect Pecan Pie Bars

Easier and better than pecan pie! This works great made a day ahead as well.

Crust:
1 ½ sticks (or ¾ cup) unsalted butter, cold and cubed
1 ½ cups flour
⅔ cup brown sugar, firmly packed
1 teaspoon salt

Filling:
½ cup unsalted butter, softened
¾ cup brown sugar, firmly packed
¼ cup white sugar
⅓ light corn syrup
¼ cup flour
2 ½ cups pecans, coarsely chopped
Pinch of salt

Preheat oven to 350°. Line a 9x13-inch pan with foil then spray the foil. In a food processor, blend together flour, sugar, butter and salt until the mixture resembles coarse sand. Add two tablespoons cold water and mix until the dough just holds together. Press dough into bottom of pan and bake 22 minutes. Beat the butter, brown sugar, white sugar and pinch of salt until light and fluffy. Add the corn syrup, flour and pecans and mix until just combined. Crumble this evenly over the crust and bake 30 minutes. When done, allow it to cool completely in the pan. Make sure you remove any foil that sticks to the bars before cutting.

Nutty Cheesecake Squares

This is so delicious and rich. To vary it, change up the kind of chips you use.

2 ½ cups graham cracker crumbs
¾ cup (or 1 ½ sticks) butter, melted
¾ cup white sugar, divided
1 cup chocolate chips
1 cup peanut butter chips
2 - 8 ounce packages cream cheese, softened
¼ cup flour
1 tablespoon vanilla extract
4 large eggs

Preheat oven to 325°. Mix the chocolate and peanut butter chips together and set aside. Mix together with a fork the graham cracker crumbs, butter and ¼ cup sugar. Reserve one cup of this for the topping. Press remaining crumb mix into ungreased 9x13-inch pan. Sprinkle half the chip mixture over that. Beat cream cheese, remaining sugar, flour, and vanilla together until smooth. Add eggs, beating well then pour that evenly over chips in the pan. Sprinkle with the remaining chips and remaining crumb mixture. Bake for 30-35 minutes. Cool completely then refrigerate until firm and cut into small bars.

```
                        Food Fact:
    Every American eats an average of 51 pounds of chocolate
                         per year.
```

Gooey Chocolate Coconut Bars

Gooey, chewy, yummy and better as the days go by.

½ cup butter
1 sleeve saltine crackers, crushed
1 cup sweetened, flaked coconut
1 cup chocolate chips
1 - 14 ounce can sweetened condensed milk
1 cup walnuts, chopped

Preheat oven to 350°. Spray all four sides of an 8X8-inch baking pan with cooking spray. Melt butter & add crackers & press firmly down into the pan. Sprinkle coconut, chips and nuts evenly over that. Pour condensed milk over it all and bake for 30 minutes.

Coconut Chew Squares

Two ingredients combine for the best and easiest treat on the planet. It is also great for company that drops by unexpectedly. It takes minutes to make and it is yummy!

5 ½ cups sweetened, flaked coconut
1 - 14 ounce can sweetened condensed milk
1 cup chocolate chips (optional)

Preheat oven to 350°. Combine the condensed milk and coconut then press it into an 8X8-inch pan that has been sprayed with nonstick cooking spray. Press firmly, making sure the top is even and flat. Bake for 40 minutes. The edges will get darker and that's the way it should be. If you decide to add chocolate chips, when the 40 minutes are over, remove the pan from the oven, sprinkle chips evenly over the top, put back in the oven for two minutes, then remove the pan and spread chips over the entire surface with a spatula. The chocolate will harden faster if you put it in the refrigerator for a little while. Chips or not, cool the pan slightly before cutting. It's great warm cold or room temperature.

Laughin' Lemon Bars

This is the ultimate tangy lemon bar; pucker up!

1 cup butter, softened
2 cups white sugar
2 cups flour
¼ teaspoon salt
4 eggs
¼ cup plus 1 tablespoon flour
⅔ cup lemon juice
Zest of 2 lemons (zest the lemons before you juice them)
Powdered sugar to taste

Preheat oven to 350°. Blend together butter, two cups flour, ½ cup white sugar and salt. Press into the bottom of an ungreased 9x13-inch pan. This step is easier if you add a small amount of flour on top of the dough before you press into the pan. Bake for 15-20 minutes or until golden. In another bowl mix 1 ½ cups white sugar and ¼ cup plus one tablespoon flour. Add eggs, lemon juice and zest and pour over the crust. Bake for 20-25 minutes. Bars firm up as they cool. When they are totally cooled, you can dust liberally with powdered sugar.

Fantastic Freezer Bars

These are not baked and you store them in your freezer; very tasty and good for you too!

1 cup peanut butter
⅔ cup honey
¼ teaspoon vanilla extract
3 tablespoons unsweetened cocoa powder
2 cups oats (quick or old-fashioned)

Spray a small baking dish or an 8X8-inch baking pan with non stick cooking spray. Melt honey and peanut butter over low. Add vanilla and cocoa powder and mix until smooth. Add oats to that then pour in pan. Dip your fingers in water and press mixture evenly into pan. Cover and place in freezer for two hours.

Pumpkin Pie Bars

Perfect for the holidays instead of traditional pumpkin pie. My husband thinks these are better.

1 ⅓ cups flour
½ cup brown sugar, firmly packed
¾ cup white sugar, divided
¾ cup cold butter
1 cup rolled oats, uncooked (quick or old-fashioned)
½ cup pecans, chopped
8 ounces cream cheese, softened
3 eggs
1 - 15 ounce can pumpkin (not pumpkin pie mix)
1 tablespoon pumpkin pie spice

Preheat oven to 350°. Line 9x13-inch pan with foil and spray it with cooking spray. Mix flour, brown sugar and ¼ cup of white sugar then cut in butter until it resembles coarse crumbs. Stir in oats and pecans. Reserve one cup of the oat mix and firmly press the remaining mixture into bottom of pan. Bake 15 minutes. Beat cream cheese, remaining ½ cup sugar, eggs, pumpkin and pumpkin pie spice until well blended. Pour over crust; sprinkle with reserved crumbs. Bake 25-30 minutes.

Chocolate Oat Goodness Bars

Heavy, dense, wonderful and kid approved as well.

½ cup butter, softened

⅓ cup white sugar

½ cup brown sugar, firmly packed

1 egg

¾ cup peanut butter

½ teaspoon vanilla extract

¾ cup flour

¼ cup oat bran (process rolled oats to powder in a blender)

1 cup rolled oats (quick or old-fashioned)

½ teaspoon baking soda

¼ teaspoon salt

¾ cup semi sweet chocolate chips

Preheat oven to 350°. In a large bowl, beat butter with sugars until smooth. Beat in egg, peanut butter and vanilla until well blended. In another bowl, whisk together flours, oat bran, oats, baking soda and salt; mix into butter mixture until smooth. Stir in chocolate chips and spread dough evenly in a buttered 8X8-inch baking pan. Bake until pale golden brown, 25-30 minutes. Let cool 10 minutes, cut into 12 pieces then let cool completely.

```
                            Food Fact:
The honeybee's brain is the size of a sesame seed, yet it has
  remarkable capacity to learn and remember things and it is
     able to make complex calculations on distance traveled.
```

Chewy Jam Bars

The oat crust in this is absolutely wonderful. This is a treat you will make over and over again. Great cold from the refrigerator as well.

1 ½ cups jam or preserves, any kind you like.
1 ¾ cups flour
1 cup brown sugar, firmly packed
½ teaspoon salt
¾ teaspoon baking soda
1 ¾ cups old-fashioned oats
1 cup walnuts, coarsely chopped
1 cup unsalted butter, melted
1 egg, beaten
1 teaspoon vanilla extract

Preheat oven to 350°. Put a piece of parchment paper in the bottom of a 9x13-inch pan then spray that and the sides with cooking spray. In a large bowl, whisk the flour, sugar, salt and baking soda. Stir in the oats and walnuts. Add the butter, egg and vanilla and mix completely. Using your fingers, press half of the crust mixture into the bottom of the pan. Spread the filling over the crust. Crumble the rest of the crust mixture on top of the jam and gently press to flatten. Don't worry if some of the jam is exposed. Bake until light golden, 35-40 minutes. Cool for one hour then cut into bars.

Chocolate Pudding Cake

One of my husband's favorite recipes and you can make it a day ahead too.

1 - 18.25 ounce box yellow cake mix
2 - 5.1 ounce boxes chocolate instant pudding
2 cups milk
1 cup powdered sugar
1 teaspoon vanilla extract

Prepare cake according to package directions and bake in a buttered 9x13-inch pan. When the cake is done, pokes holes into it with the handle of a wooden spoon. The more holes you poke the better! Set the cake aside then mix together pudding, vanilla, sugar and milk, beating for one minute on medium speed, scraping down sides of the bowl as needed. Immediately pour half of that evenly over the warm cake and set aside. Put the remaining pudding in the refrigerator for 10 minutes, then spread it evenly on the cake. Chill for an hour and you will have a party in your mouth!

The Best Chocolate Cake Ever

It took me years to come up with this cake; so moist, it doesn't get dry in the fridge. It is best made a day ahead then frost it the next day with my Classic Butter Cream Frosting.

2 cups white sugar
1 ¾ cups flour
1 cup unsweetened cocoa powder
1 ½ teaspoons baking powder
1 ½ teaspoons baking soda
1 teaspoon salt
2 eggs
1 cup milk
½ cup olive oil (light, regular or extra-virgin all work)
2 teaspoons vanilla extract
1 cup boiling water

Preheat oven to 350°. Grease and flour either a 9x13-inch pan, two round pans or three round pans. In bowl mix sugar, flour, cocoa, baking powder, baking soda and salt. Add eggs, milk, oil and vanilla; mix until smooth then stir in water. Batter will be quite thin. Spray pan or pans well with cooking spray, add batter and bake. If you use a 9x13-inch pan, it takes 40 minutes, two round pans take 35 minutes and three round pans take 25 minutes.

Classic Butter Cream Frosting

Easy to make and even easier to devour!

1 cup butter, softened
2 teaspoons vanilla extract
2 ½ cups powdered sugar
¼ cup milk

Beat butter, sugar and vanilla till creamy then add milk and mix on high for several minutes until completely smooth.

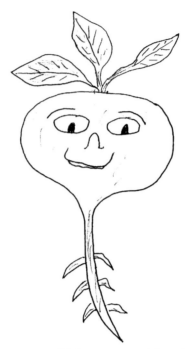

Chocolate Beet Cake

Kids love this and adults too and no one will have any idea it contains beets.

1 - 15 ounce can beets (not pickled), drained but save ½ cup of juice
1 ½ cups white sugar
½ cup olive oil (light, regular or extra-virgin all work)
3 eggs
1 teaspoon vanilla extract
1 ½ cups flour
¾ cup unsweetened cocoa powder
1 ½ teaspoons baking soda
½ teaspoon salt
¾ cup semi sweet chocolate chips

Preheat oven to 350°. Puree beets in a food processor or blender with the reserved beet juice until smooth. Then combine beets to sugar, oil, eggs and vanilla. In another bowl combine flour, cocoa, soda and salt. Add that to beet mixture and mix well. Pour into three greased 8x4x2-inch pans, ¾ full (I use the disposable aluminum ones). Sprinkle ¼ cup of chocolate chips over each ne and push them into the batter with a knife so they are hidden. Bake for 40 inutes. *To make a 3 layer cake, double the recipe and bake in 3, 9-inch cake pans for 40 minutes as well.

Flourless Chocolate Cake

The missing flour makes this very creamy inside. Very rich with deep chocolate flavor.

4 ounces semi sweet chocolate, chopped
½ cup butter
¾ cup white sugar
½ cup cocoa powder
3 eggs, beaten
1 teaspoon vanilla extract

Preheat oven to 300°. Grease an 8 or 9-inch round cake pan, line it with parchment paper and dust that with cocoa powder. In double boiler (or glass bowl set over a pan of lightly boiling water), melt chocolate and butter. Remove from heat; stir in sugar, cocoa powder, eggs and vanilla. Pour into prepared pan and bake 30 minutes. Serve it warm or let it cool completely.

Table Tippin' Dump Cake

From my radio friend Rollin's wife, Anita. Whenever I bring this to a potluck m *is the first thing gone and people always ask for the recipe.*

1 - 20 ounce can crushed pineapple and its juice
1 - 20 ounce can cherry pie filling
1 - 18.25 ounce box yellow cake mix
¾ cup butter, melted
1 cup unsalted nuts, chopped
Sweetened, flaked coconut to taste

Preheat oven to 350°. Grease a 9x13-inch pan. Dump into that the crushed pineapple and its juice and spread evenly. Next add pie filling and spread evenly. Sprinkle the entire thing with the cake mix, don't break up the clumps. On top of that pour the butter, then the nuts, ending with enough coconut to cover. Bake for 45 minutes. At 35 minutes cover it loosely with foil so the coconut doesn't burn.

Sweetheart's Almond Cake

Mary Todd Lincoln made this often while dating soon-to-be President Abraham Lincoln. He said it was the best cake he ever ate. After they married, it was served at many White House dinners.

1 cup butter, softened
1 cup blanched almonds (skinless almonds)
2 cups plus 2 tablespoons white sugar
3 cups flour
1 tablespoon baking powder
1 cup milk
6 cold egg whites
1 teaspoon vanilla extract
1 pint strawberries, washed and sliced
Sweetened whipped cream

Preheat oven to 350°. Grease and flour a 9x13-inch pan. In a food processor or blender, process almonds until they resemble coarse flour. Beat butter and sugar until they are light and fluffy. Sift flour and baking powder three times. Fold flour mixture into butter mixture, alternating with milk, until well blended. Stir in almonds and mix well. Beat egg whites until they form stiff peaks. Fold the egg whites gently into butter mixture. Add vanilla until incorporated. Bake one hour or until a skewer inserted comes out clean. Toss strawberries with two tablespoons white sugar and set aside. When the cake has cooled to room temperature, serve each piece with a dollop of whipped cream then top with the strawberry/sugar mixture.

Barb's Rhubarb Cake

Another great dish we had growing up!

2 cups rhubarb, cut in ½-inch slices
2 cups brown sugar, firmly packed
½ cup butter, softened
2 eggs
1 teaspoon baking soda
1 cup buttermilk
2 cups flour
½ teaspoon salt

Mix sugar and butter till creamy. Add eggs and buttermilk and mix well. In another bowl mix soda, flour and salt. Fold in rhubarb and pour mixture into 9x13-inch pan. Evenly sprinkle topping mixture evenly over that and bake 40-45 minutes.

Topping:
¼ cup white sugar
½ teaspoon ground cinnamon

Mix together and set aside.

Pecan Cream Cheese Frosting

Rich and smooth, this is good on everything from cakes to your finger.

8 ounces cream cheese, softened
½ cup butter, softened
2 ½ cups powdered sugar
2 teaspoons vanilla extract
1 cup pecans, finely chopped

Beat cream cheese, butter, sugar and vanilla until smooth then stir in nuts.

Caramel Pineapple Cake

My friend Kathleen made this for me one night and I just had to have the recipe! It is so rich and chewy.

¼ cup plus 2 tablespoons butter
½ cup brown sugar, firmly packed
1 - 15 ¼ ounce can sliced pineapple (save ¼ cup of the juice)
2 eggs
1 cup white sugar
1 cup flour
1 teaspoon baking powder
¼ teaspoon salt
¼ cup pineapple juice
Walnut halves, as many as you want

In a 10-inch cast iron or oven proof skillet, melt butter and brown sugar and cook for 5 minutes, stirring often. Add 7 pineapple rings to the bottom of the skillet and put walnuts between each. Beat eggs and sugar until fluffy then mix in pineapple juice. Add flour, baking powder and salt; mix well and pour batter in pineapple lined skillet. Bake uncovered at 350° for 30 minutes then cover with foil and bake 5 minutes longer. Loosen sides with a knife, let it sit for 5 minutes then turn upside down on to a serving plate very carefully as it is very hot.

Coconut Cake with Lemon Filling

Moist cake, rich lemon filling, cream cheese frosted with coconut. Make the frosting first and put it in the freezer for 30 minutes so it is easier to work with.

Frosting:
1 ½ packages (12 ounces) cream cheese, softened
½ cup butter, softened
1 ½ teaspoons vanilla extract
3 cups powdered sugar
Sweetened, flaked coconut to garnish

Beat cream cheese, butter and vanilla. When smooth, slowly beat in the powdered sugar. Set aside.

Cake:
1 cup butter, softened
2 cups white sugar
3 eggs
2 teaspoons vanilla extract
3 ¼ cups flour
3 ¼ teaspoons baking powder
¾ teaspoon salt
1 ½ cups milk

In a large bowl, beat together butter and sugar. Add eggs one at a time, beating after each then add vanilla. Combine flour, baking powder and salt and add to creamed mixture alternately with milk. Pour into three greased, floured and parchment lined 9-inch round pans and bake at 350° for 25-30 minutes.

Filling:
1 cup white sugar
¼ cup cornstarch
1 cup water
4 egg yolks, beaten
⅓ cup lemon juice
2 tablespoons butter

Have all of these elements ready to go before you start. In small pan, combine sugar, cornstarch and water. Bring to boil and cook two minutes; stirring constantly. Remove from heat and stir a small amount of this hot mixture into the egg yolks. Then return egg mixture back to the pan and boil gently for two minutes. Add lemon juice and butter ; mix well. Pour into a bowl and let set to room temperature. Place one cake on a plate and top that with half the lemon filling. Add the next cake and cover with the remaining lemon filling. Add final cake and frost the top first then the sides. Then cover the whole cake with as much coconut as you can get on it. The more, the better!

7 Up Cake

A recipe from 1957. You'll be amazed at how light and airy the 7 Up makes the cake.

1 - 18.25 ounce box yellow cake mix
4 eggs
¼ cup olive oil (light, regular or extra-virgin all work)
½ cup applesauce
1 - 3.4 ounce box instant vanilla pudding
10 ounces of 7 Up

Preheat oven to 350°. Mix all ingredients together well. Pour into a 9x13-inch pan that has been sprayed with cooking spray. Bake 40 minutes and let cool.

Frosting:
1 cup white sugar
½ cup crushed pineapple, drained
¼ cup butter
2 tablespoons flour
2 eggs, beaten
1 cup sweetened, flaked coconut (optional)

Mix together sugar, pineapple, butter and flour and cook for 5 minutes. Take a bit of the pineapple mixture and add it to the beaten eggs so the hot mixture doesn't scramble the eggs. Then add all of the egg mixture back into the pineapple mixture and whisk until it thickens. Remove from heat and stir in coconut (if using). Set aside to cool. When it is completely cool, frost the cake.

Sweet Potato Cake

My cousin Jill gave me this recipe and I absolutely loved it! This melt-in-your-mouth cake is so moist and the longer it sits in your refrigerator; the better it gets.

1 ¾ cups white sugar
¾ cup olive oil (light, regular or extra-virgin all work)
3 eggs
1 teaspoon vanilla extract
2 cups sweet potatoes, cooked and mashed (you can also use canned)
2 cups flour
3 teaspoons baking powder
2 teaspoons baking soda
¼ teaspoon salt
½ teaspoon ground ginger
½ cup beer, regular or non alcoholic

Preheat oven to 350°. Cover a 9x13-inch pan with cooking spray. Combine sugar and oil then beat in eggs, vanilla and potatoes. Combine flour, baking powder, baking soda and salt in a separate bowl; stir into sweet potato mixture, alternating with beer until everything is just combined. Do not over mix. Bake 40-45 minutes. Put the icing on right when it comes out of the oven. If you make the cake a day ahead, save the icing to put on the next day.

Icing:
¾ cup powdered sugar
¾ cup brown sugar, firmly packed
½ cup heavy cream
¼ cup butter
¼ teaspoon vanilla extract

In a pan, add brown sugar, cream and butter over medium-low heat ur sugar dissolves then boil the mixture for three minutes, stirring occasic Remove from heat, add vanilla then slowly pour over the powdered sugar and whisk it all until very smooth.

Cherry Pretzel Cheesecake

Super easy and the pretzel crust gives it just the right salty/sweet combination.

1 ½ cups pretzels, crushed

¾ cup white sugar, divided

½ cup butter, melted

2 - 8 ounce packages cream cheese, softened

1 - 14 ounce can sweetened condensed milk

3 eggs

¼ cup lemon juice plus 1 tablespoon

1 cup sour cream

2 or 3 - 21 ounce cans of cherry pie filling (I say the more the better!)

Preheat oven to 300°. Combine pretzels and sugar then stir in the butter. Press into a 9x13-inch pan. Beat cream cheese until fluffy and gradually beat in milk until smooth. Add eggs, sugar and lemon juice and mix well. Pour onto pretzel crust and bake 45-50 minutes or until center is set. Remove from oven then top with sour cream and bake 5 minutes more. Cool on counter for one hour then add the pie filling evenly on top and chill at least four hours. You can also make it a day ahead.

Limey Lime Cake

This is tangy and moist and the best lime cake you'll ever have! Our friends Kelly and Jewel say it makes their "eyes sweat" cause it is so full of lime flavor. Try slicing the cake with unflavored, waxed dental floss, it will make neater slices than a knife. I put the frosting in the freezer for an hour before using so it is easier to work with.

1 - 18.25 ounce box lemon cake mix
¾ cup applesauce
⅓ cup plus 4 tablespoons olive oil (light, regular or extra-virgin all work)
4 eggs
1 - 3 ounce package lime gelatin
¾ cup orange juice
½ cup lime juice
½ cup powdered sugar

Preheat oven to 325°. Combine cake mix, gelatin, applesauce, oil, eggs and orange juice. Heavily spray three round cake pans with baking spray, equally pour batter into all three pans and bake for 28 minutes. While they bake, combine lime juice and powdered sugar; set aside. When the cakes come out of the oven, poke holes all over into each one with a fork then drizzle each with lime juice mixture and set them aside.

Frosting:
½ cup butter, softened
8 ounces cream cheese, softened
1 teaspoon vanilla extract
Zest of 2 limes (zest the limes before you juice them)
6 tablespoons lime juice
4 cups powdered sugar

For the frosting, beat the butter and cream cheese until smooth. Add lime juice, zest and powdered sugar and mix well. Make sure the cakes are totally cooled before frosting. There is enough frosting to put a good amount between each layer as well as frost the entire cake.

Raspberry Lemon Angel Food Cake

I made this for our bible study group who loved it, so I just had to add it in my book.

1 – 16 ounce package angel food cake mix
2 large lemons and their zest (zest the lemons before you juice them)
2 cups powdered sugar
8 ounces frozen whipped topping, thawed (I like Cool Whip)
1 – 12 ounce package frozen raspberries, thawed

Preheat oven to 350°. Prepare cake mix according to package directions then pour batter into ungreased 9x13-inch pan. Bake for 40 minutes on center rack. The crust will be a deep golden brown, cracked and firm to the touch. Cool it completely in pan then poke holes in cake every inch using a wooden skewer. In a small bowl mix lemon juice, zest and powdered sugar, then pour evenly over cake. There are two ways to finish this. Evenly place raspberries on top of cake, cover with whipped topping and chill for a few hours or fold raspberries into whipped topping, spread that evenly over cake and chill for a few hours.

Odessa Waffle's Butter Cake

A great treat that's gooey and rich and wonderful served at room temperature or cold.

1 - 18.25 ounce box yellow cake mix
½ cup butter, melted
1 egg, beaten
8 ounces cream cheese, softened
2 eggs
2 cups powdered sugar (plus more for garnish)
2 cups pecans, chopped
¾ cup sweetened, flaked coconut (optional)

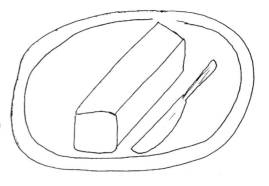

Mix cake mix, butter and one beaten egg and spread into a 9x13-inch pan that has been coated with cooking spray. Mix together cream cheese, two eggs and powdered sugar. Spread over top of cake batter. Bake at 350° for 40 minutes. Remove from oven, sprinkle with powdered sugar, pecans and the optional coconut. Cool completely. Liberally dust with powdered sugar before serving.

Classic Carrot Cake

I put the frosting in the freezer for an hour so it is easier to work with. I use two spoons at the same time to put the frosting on as it works much better than a knife and you can catch falling frosting a lot easier too!

4 ½ cups flour
1 tablespoon and 1 teaspoon baking soda
1 tablespoon and 1 teaspoon ground cinnamon
2 teaspoons pumpkin pie spice
2 teaspoons baking powder
2 teaspoons salt
1 ½ cups brown sugar, firmly packed
1 ½ cups white sugar
6 eggs
2 teaspoons vanilla extract
2 cups olive oil (light, regular or extra-virgin all work)
4 cups carrots, grated
1 - 28 ounce canned crushed pineapple, drained
1 cup golden raisins
2 cups pecans, chopped

Preheat oven to 350°. Mix flour, baking soda, cinnamon, pumpkin pie spice, baking powder and salt. In another larger bowl, mix sugar and eggs then add vanilla and oil. Mix wet to dry then add carrots, pineapple, raisins and nuts. Pour evenly into three round well greased pans that have parchment paper in the bottom. Bake 40 minutes. It is done when a toothpick inserted in the center comes out clean. Depending on your oven, you may need to cook the cakes 5-10 minutes longer. Let cake cool completely before frosting. To keep the layers from slipping out of place, before frosting, I put in three wood skewers in the stack then cut them off at the cake line.

Frosting:
3 - 8 ounce packages cream cheese, softened
1 cup butter, softened
3 teaspoons vanilla extract
5 cups powdered sugar

Beat cream cheese and butter until well mixed then add vanilla. Slowly add sugar till it is smooth. Place some frosting between each layer then frost the entire cake.

Pistachio Walnut Cake

I can't say enough about how amazing this cake is. The green color makes for a nice surprise when you cut into it. It is a cake that you will share over and over again.

1 - 18.25 ounce package white cake mix
3 eggs
¾ cup vegetable oil
1 cup lemon-lime soft drink
1 - 3 ounce package instant pistachio pudding mix
1 cup sweetened, flaked coconut
¾ cup chopped pecans

Combine cake mix, oil, eggs, soft drink and pudding for 5 minutes. Fold in the coconut and pecans. Pour into greased and floured 9x13-inch pan. Bake at 350° for 45 minutes. Cool then add icing.

Icing:
2 - 1.3 ounce envelopes whipped topping mix (I use Dream Whip)
1 - 3 ounce package instant pistachio pudding mix
1 ½ cups milk
¾ cup chopped walnuts
½ cup sweetened, flaked coconut

Combine whipped topping mix, milk, and pudding. Beat until thick then spread over cake. Sprinkle walnuts and coconut evenly on top of that.

Classic Pound Cake

This is rich and dense and is a great foundation for strawberry shortcake. It is even a good breakfast, toasted in the toaster smeared with lots of butter and jam.

2 cups butter, softened
3 cups white sugar
6 eggs
4 cups flour
1 cup milk
1 teaspoon almond extract
1 teaspoon vanilla extract

Cream butter and add sugar. Continue beating adding one egg at a time. Add flour alternately with milk; begin & end with flour. Stir in flavorings. Put the batter into two loaf pans that have been sprayed well with cooking spray. Bake at 325° for one hour and 10 minutes or until a toothpick inserted near the center comes out clean. Cool for 15 minutes before removing from the pan.

Sweet Crispix Mix

My brother-in-law Mark's mom Trudy has been making this during the holidays for years. I was very thankful when she let me have the recipe for my cookbook!

10 cups Crispix cereal
1 large jar roasted and salted peanuts,
½ cup butter
¾ cup brown sugar, firmly packed
¼ cup light corn syrup

Preheat oven to 250°. Put cereal and peanuts into a large brown paper bag from the grocery store. In saucepan mix butter, sugar and corn syrup and boil that for 5 minutes. Pour over cereal mixture and shake in bag until the cereal and nuts are coated. Pour onto a baking sheet and bake for 15 minutes or till the mixture is completely dry.

Sopapilla Cheesecake

Better than regular cheesecake and a million times easier! An 'must try' recipe!

3 - 8 ounce packages cream cheese, softened
2 cups white sugar
1 egg
1 ½ teaspoons vanilla extract
2 - 8 ounce cans crescent rolls (I use the full sheets so I don't have to press the perforations together and they spread easier if used at room temperature)
½ cup butter, melted
1 teaspoon ground cinnamon
¼ cup sliced almonds

Preheat oven to 350°. Beat the cream cheese, 1 ½ cups sugar, egg and the vanilla until smooth. Unroll the cans of crescent roll dough and use a rolling pin, shape each piece into a 9x13-inch rectangle. Press one of the pieces into the bottom of an ungreased 9x13-inch pan. Evenly spread the cream cheese mixture on top of that then cover with the remaining piece of crescent dough. Pour melted butter evenly over the top of that. Stir the remaining ½ cup of sugar together with the cinnamon in a small bowl then sprinkle it over the cheesecake along with the almonds. Bake until the dough has puffed and turned golden, about 45 minutes. Cool completely in the pan before cutting.

Peanut Butter Planets

My husbands' grandma made these every Christmas. They take some time as this recipe makes a lot but these melt-in-your-mouth treats are well worth it!

½ cup butter, melted
18 ounces creamy peanut butter
2 teaspoons vanilla extract
3 cups powdered sugar
3 ¼ cups Rice Krispies
1 ½ packages (18 ounces) semi sweet chocolate chips
3 tablespoons coconut oil (at health food stores; can also use shortening)

Melt butter then stir in peanut butter, vanilla, powdered sugar and Rice Krispies. Mix well, chill until its cooled then roll into marble sized balls. In a double boiler (or glass bowl over simmering water) on low heat, melt the coconut oil (or shortening) with the chocolate chips. Dip peanut butter balls into chocolate chip mixture using tooth picks until they're well coated. Remove with tooth picks onto waxed paper. These rarely look perfectly round and that is how they are supposed to be.

Tantalizing Truffles

These are super rich and the Bailey's Irish Cream is what 'makes' them. I've even used a generic brand and they come out just as good!

½ cup Bailey's Irish Cream
¼ cup heavy cream
1 tablespoon butter, melted
12 ounces semi sweet chocolate
2 egg yolks

Melt chocolate, Bailey's Irish Cream and heavy cream over low. Whisk in yolks, one at a time then add butter. To firm it up so it rolls easier, put this mixture in the refrigerator for a few hours. Take it out, make marble sized balls and roll them in cocoa powder *or* toasted chopped nuts *or* toasted sweetened, flaked coconut *or* chocolate sprinkles. You decide!

Grandma Verna's Toffee

My husband's grandma was known for these during the holidays. Make extra as they disappear fast. They are totally different tasting cold as opposed to room temperature but both are equally good!

1 cup brown sugar, firmly packed
1 cup butter, softened
1 egg yolk
1 teaspoon vanilla extract
1 cup flour
⅛ teaspoon salt
2 cups nuts, rough chopped and any kind you like
1 ½ cups semi sweet chocolate chips

Line a large jelly roll pan (17 ½-inch x 12 ½-inch) with foil that drapes over the edges then spray the foil with cooking spray. Mix brown sugar, butter, egg yolk, vanilla, flour and salt. Place dough in large blobs around the pan. Sprinkle some flour on top of each blob and press them out so dough covers the whole bottom of the pan, going all the way to the edges. Use as much flour as you need to help it spread easier. Bake for 15 minutes at 350° then remove from oven, sprinkle the whole thing with chocolate chips and put it back in for two minutes. Remove from the oven, spread the chocolate across the dough like frosting. Add nuts, pushing them into the dough with a spoon or spatula. Let harden and crack off into the size of pieces you like.

The Bee's Knees Candy

This is really healthy, simple and good!

¼ cup coconut oil (at health food stores; can also use shortening)
3 tablespoons honey
½ teaspoon vanilla extract
¼ cup unsweetened cocoa powder
½ cup almonds, chopped
Pinch of salt

Melt coconut oil and honey in pan over medium-low heat. Then add salt, vanilla, cocoa powder; stir till well mixed. Add almonds then pour into a loaf pan that has been lined with parchment paper. Place in freezer for at least two hours. Transfer to a cutting board and chop into pieces.
Store in the freezer.

Carob Freezer Candy

Good for you and good for people who can't eat dairy products.

1 cup raw cashews
¼ cup water
3 tablespoons honey
2 tablespoons carob powder
1 teaspoon vanilla extract
¼ teaspoon salt

Blend well in blender or a high speed blender (I like Vitamix or Blendtec) and pour in a flat dish. Put it in the freezer until it sets up. You must store in the freezer as well.

Chocolate Coconut Macaroons

These keep for a long time in the refrigerator. They are really yummy!

1 - 14 ounce can sweetened condensed milk
8 ounces sweetened, flaked coconut
3 ounces unsweetened chocolate
1 teaspoon vanilla extract
Pinch of salt

Preheat oven to 350°. Mix milk, salt, and chocolate in a double boiler, stirring frequently. When chocolate has melted, add coconut and vanilla. Grease baking sheets. Drop mixture by the spoonful on cookie sheets about an inch apart. Bake for 13 minutes. At room temperature, the insides will remind you of truffles and when they are cold they seem like a whole different cookie. Both are excellent though!

Four Ingredient Cookies

These melt in your mouth and you always have the ingredients on hand.

1 cup butter, softened
½ cup white sugar
2 cups pecans, finely chopped (can also use walnuts)
2 cups flour

Preheat oven to 350°. Spray baking sheets with cooking spray. Beat butter and sugar until creamy. Stir in nuts and flour. Bake 14-15 minutes.

Dough Wrangler Cookies

Growing up my mom always made these with her extra pie dough. Rolled thin; these are flaky, delicate and crunchy. Our 3 dogs Malchus, Ruby and Pal love them too!

One order of my Perfect Pie Crust recipe
White sugar and cinnamon to taste

Roll the dough out, using flour as needed to stop it from sticking. Cut rough pieces by hand or use a cookie cutter and place the cookies on a ungreased baking sheet. Sprinkle with sugar and cinnamon to taste. Bake them at 350° for 20-25 minutes.

Best Ever Oatmeal Cookies

The best. Period!

3 cups old-fashioned oats
2 cups brown sugar, firmly packed
1 cup unsalted butter, softened
2 eggs
2 teaspoons vanilla
1 teaspoon baking soda
½ teaspoon salt
1 ½ cups flour

Preheat oven to 375°. Beat butter and sugar. Add vanilla, oats, eggs, flour, soda and salt; mix well. Stir in flour. Use a mini-ice cream scoop and drop lightly greased sheets. Bake 9 minutes. Let stand one minute before removing from pan.

Iced Orange Chocolate Chip Cookies

This recipe is from my sister-in-law Susan and one of the best cookies I've ever had. We like them best iced and really cold. My husband prefers these without the icing.

1 cup butter, softened
1 cup white sugar
3 ounces cream cheese, softened
2 eggs
2 teaspoons orange juice
Zest of 1 orange (zest before you juice)
2 ¼ cups flour
¼ teaspoon salt
12 ounces semi sweet chocolate chips

Preheat oven to 350°. Grease cookie sheets lightly. Beat butter, sugar and cream cheese. Add eggs, juice and lemon zest. Add flour and salt then fold in the chocolate chips. Place parchment paper on a cookie sheet. Form the dough into rounded teaspoonfuls and place them on the parchment paper, two inches apart. Bake 12-15 minutes or until lightly browned around the edge. Add icing when they're completely cool. *The great thing about using parchment paper to bake cookies and not cooking spray is you can save your sheets of parchment paper and use them time and time again.

Icing:
2 cups powdered sugar
3 ounces cream cheese, softened
1 teaspoon orange juice
Zest of 1 orange

Mix powdered sugar, cream cheese, orange juice and zest until creamy.

Chewy Cream Cheese Cookies

They are super chewy and easy to make and just as good without the nuts.

1 cup butter, softened
6 ounces cream cheese, softened
2 cups flour
1 ¼ cups white sugar
1 cup walnuts or pecans, chopped

Preheat oven to 350°. Beat butter and cream cheese. Then beat in flour, sugar and nuts. This dough is very dry and it will take a few minutes to come together, but it will. Place tablespoons of dough on an ungreased cookie sheet, two inches apart. I use a mini ice cream scoop so all the cookies are the same size. Bake 15-17 minutes. Right when you take them out of the oven, press each cookie flat with a spatula, then let them cool on the pan a few minutes before removing.

Best Ever Chocolate Chip Cookies

AMAZING and if you make them with carob chips, your dog will love them too!

6 ounces cream cheese, softened
¾ cup unsalted butter, melted
1 cup brown sugar, firmly packed
½ cup white sugar
2 teaspoons vanilla extract
2 cups plus 3 tablespoons flour
½ teaspoon baking soda
¼ teaspoon plus a pinch salt
1 ½ cups chocolate chips (also try toffee chips, butterscotch, anything really!)

Preheat oven to 350°. Line a large cookie sheet with parchment paper. Beat butter, cream cheese, vanilla and sugars until fluffy. Add flour, soda and salt. Beat until well combined. Stir in chocolate chips. Place about two tablespoons on baking sheet and flatten slightly with your hand. Bake 13-16 minutes. Cool two minutes on pan.

Cranberry Orange Cookies

Tart, sweet, chewy, a hit! A mini ice cream scoop makes them all the same size.

1 cup butter, softened
1 cup white sugar
½ cup brown sugar, firmly packed
1 egg
Zest of 1 orange
2 tablespoons orange juice
2 ½ cups flour
½ teaspoon baking soda
¼ teaspoon salt
1 ½ cups dried cranberries
½ cup chopped walnuts

Preheat oven to 375°. In a large bowl, beat the butter, white sugar and brown sugar until light and fluffy. Beat in the egg then add the zest and orange juice. In another bowl, combine flour, baking soda and salt then stir it into the orange mixture. Fold in cranberries and walnuts. Drop dough by rounded tablespoonful onto ungreased cookie sheets at least two inches apart. Bake for 12 minutes. Let them cool on the pan a few minutes before you take them off. Store at room temperature or refrigerate.

Ultimate Peanut Butter Cookies

Enough said, these are the best! We like them best stored at room temperature.

1 cup butter, softened
1 cup white sugar
1 cup brown sugar, firmly packed
2 eggs
1 ½ cups peanut butter
1 teaspoon vanilla
3 cups flour
1 teaspoon baking soda
½ teaspoon salt

Preheat oven to 375°. Beat the butter and sugars until light and fluffy. Add eggs, peanut butter, vanilla and mix well. Add soda, salt and flour. Roll dough into balls, place on lightly greased sheets, make criss-cross pattern on them with a fork. Bake 9 minutes for soft cookies and 13 minutes for crispy cookies.

Lil's Ginger Cookies

My grandma stored her cookies in an old movie reel tin that I now use today.

1 ½ cups brown sugar, firmly packed
1 cup butter, softened
3 tablespoons molasses
1 egg
2 ½ cups flour
1 teaspoon ground cinnamon
½ teaspoon ground cloves
2 teaspoons baking soda
½ teaspoon ground ginger
½ teaspoon salt
White sugar for garnish

Preheat oven to 350°. Mix everything together. For each cookie, roll some dough into a ball and flatten each with a glass that was first dipped in white sugar. Bake for 8-10 minutes.

Lemon Iced Butter Cookies

A delicate, flaky cookie with a tart lemon icing. They literally melt in your mouth.

1 cup butter, softened
¾ cup powdered sugar
2 tablespoons milk
1 ½ cups flour
¾ cup cornstarch
½ cup pecans, chopped

In a large bowl, beat butter and sugar till light and fluffy, then add milk and mix until smooth. Combine flour and cornstarch; gradually add to butter mixture. Cover and refrigerate for one hour, then roll dough into one inch balls. Dip each ball halfway into pecans. Place them nut side down on ungreased baking sheets and flatten slightly. Bake at 350° for 15 minutes. Cool completely before you frost them.

Frosting:
2 ½ cups powdered sugar
3 ½ tablespoons lemon juice
Zest of 1 lemon (zest the lemon before you juice it)
1 tablespoon butter, melted

Beat all ingredients together till smooth and free of lumps. Spread a generous amount on top of each cookie.

Norwegian Black Pepper Cookies

Sounds weird but they are so good! A classic Norwegian treat at Christmas time.

1 cup and 2 tablespoons butter, softened
1 cup white sugar
¼ cup heavy cream or half-and-half (liquid non-dairy creamer also works)
1 teaspoon baking soda
3 ¼ cups flour
1 teaspoon ground cinnamon
1 teaspoon black pepper
1 ½ teaspoons ground cardamom
1 teaspoon baking powder
2 tablespoons water

Beat together the butter and the sugar until light and fluffy. Mix in the cream or half-and-half, baking soda and water. In another bowl whisk together flour, cinnamon, pepper, cardamom and baking powder then combine with the butter mixture and blend well. Separate dough in half and roll into a log that is 2 ½ inches in diameter. Wrap each log in wax paper and put them in the freezer for two hours or in the fridge overnight. To bake, cut each log into thin slices, place on baking sheets that have been sprayed with cooking spray and cook at 375° for 10-15 minutes. The crunchier they are, the better they are!

Perfect Pie Crust

This is the only pie crust I will actually eat. It is flaky and delicious with just the right amount of sugar. This recipe makes two crusts and if you only need one, the dough freezes quite well.

1 cup salted butter, cold
3 cups flour
3 tablespoons white sugar
Ice cold water (I normally use ⅓ cup. You want to add enough water until the dough just starts to clump together. The less water you use, the more flakey your crust will be. I sometimes use so little water that I have to put the dough in the pan in pieces because it is so dry it does not hold together very well. The end result is so worth it, a super flakey crust!)

Combine flour and three tablespoons sugar in a food processor. Cut butter into pieces; add it to the flour mixture and pulse together just until it is a course meal. *If you do not have a processor, cut the butter into the flour and sugar until it is a course meal.* Dump the ice out of the water and pour water in and run the processor until the dough starts to clump into a ball. *If you do not have a processor, mix water in until dough goes into a ball.* Put on lightly flowered surface and knead until it just comes together. Divide dough into two parts. Roll out dough to a large circle on a well floured board. Place one piece in a pie plate and use a fork to score the entire bottom. Put a piece of parchment paper on top of the dough then add dry beans to weight it down and bake at 425° for 10 minutes. Then remove the parchment paper and the beans and put the crust back in the oven to bake for 7-10 more minutes.

Grandma's Lemon Pie

From my Grandma Lil who taught me so much about cooking. This is the same grandma who made my brother and I eat stewed prunes every morning for 2 weeks each summer when we visited.

1 cup white sugar
2 tablespoons flour
3 tablespoons cornstarch
¼ teaspoon salt
1 ½ cups water
2 ½ lemons (zest first then juice)
2 tablespoons butter
4 egg yolks, beaten and save three egg whites for the meringue
9-inch pie crust, baked
Never Fail Meringue

In a medium saucepan, whisk together one cup white sugar, flour, cornstarch, and salt. Stir in water, lemon juice and zest. Cook over medium-high heat, stirring frequently, until mixture comes to a boil. Stir in butter. Place egg yolks in a small bowl and gradually whisk in a half cup of hot sugar mixture. Whisk egg yolk mixture back into remaining sugar mix. Bring to a boil and continue to cook while stirring constantly until it thickens. Remove from heat and pour filling into a baked pie shell. Let pie cool in refrigerator for one hour before covering with Never Fail Meringue.

Never Fail Meringue

Grandma Lil's tried and true meringue. The only one that does not pull away from the edges.

1 tablespoon cornstarch
2 tablespoons cold water
½ cup boiling water
1 teaspoon lemon juice
3 egg whites
¼ cup plus 2 tablespoons white sugar

In small saucepan over medium heat, mix cornstarch and cold water then stir in boiling water and bring it all to a boil, stirring constantly. Remove from heat and set it in a pan of cold water to cool. Beat egg whites with lemon juice until you have stiff peaks. Add the sugar gradually beating well then add cornstarch mixture and blend. Pile it on top of your pie, making sure it goes all the way to the edges of the crust and bake at 350° until lightly browned, usually about 10 minutes.

Rich Pumpkin Pie

This is from my mom and there is none better! This is rich, spicy and dark colored, the way pumpkin pie should be. This makes two very full pies.

1 - 29 ounce (or 1 pound 13 ounce) can of pumpkin
1 ½ cups white sugar
4 large eggs
2 - 12 ounce cans evaporated milk
1 teaspoon salt
4 teaspoons ground cinnamon
2 teaspoons ground ginger
½ teaspoon ground cloves
2 - 9-inch pie crusts, unbaked

Preheat oven to 425°. Mix sugar, salt, cinnamon, ginger and cloves in small bowl. Beat eggs in large bowl then stir in pumpkin and sugar-spice mixture. Gradually stir in evaporated milk. Pour into two pie shells. If you have any extra filling, you can pour it into a small oven proof dish and bake it along with the pies.) Bake pies for 15 minutes then reduce your oven temperature to 350° and bake 45-50 minutes or until knife in center comes out clean. Cool for two hours on wire rack before serving.

```
Food Fact:
In early colonial times, pumpkins were used as an ingredient
          for the crust of pies, not the filling.
```

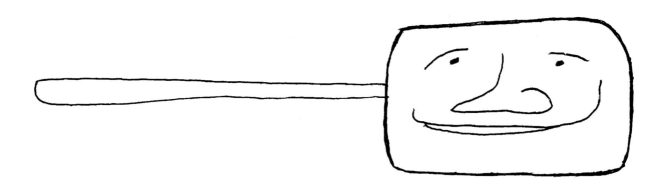

French Silk Pie

My friend Jewel said this is better that the French Silk she's had at a place famous for their pies. What a nice compliment! You can make this a day ahead too. It does take some extra time to make due to beating the eggs but it is so, so, so, worth it!

3 - 1 ounce squares unsweetened chocolate
1 cup unsalted butter, softened
1 cup white sugar
½ teaspoon vanilla extract
4 eggs (the larger the eggs, the more filling you'll get)
9-inch pie crust, baked and cooled completely
1 chocolate bar, grated (I say the more the better!)
Sweetened whipped cream for garnish

In a pan, melt chocolate over low heat then set aside. Beat butter and sugar until pale yellow and light and fluffy. This is a very important step or your filling will not increase enough. Add chocolate and vanilla to butter mixture. Add eggs one at a time, beating on high 5 full minutes after each. This is also a very important step or you will not get the filling volume you will need. Pour into a baked pie shell and in put in the refrigerator at least two hours to set. After the pie is set, garnish with by sprinkling the entire pie with the Grated chocolate bar and add a spoonful of whipped cream on each piece. I also sometimes cover the entire pie with whipped cream then sprinkle the chocolate over that.

Goober Pie

Rich and creamy; it'll remind you of pecan pie but it is a nice change. Salty peanuts paired with sweet, sticky filling will have you making this often.

2 eggs, beaten
⅓ cup creamy peanut butter
⅓ cup white sugar
⅓ cup light corn syrup
⅓ cup dark corn syrup
½ cup butter, melted
1 teaspoon vanilla extract
¾ cup salted peanuts, rough chopped
9-inch pie crust, unbaked

Preheat oven to 375°. Blend eggs, peanut butter, sugar, corn syrups, butter and vanilla. Fold in the nuts and pour in crust. Place pie on a cookie sheet and bake for 50 minutes. This is best to eat when it has cooled a bit.

Food Fact:
Someone once pushed a peanut to the top of the 14,100 foot Pike's Peak using just his nose. It took 4 days.

Graham Cracker Crust

This it the perfect mix and it does not need sugar.

1 ½ cups graham cracker crumbs
½ cup butter, melted

Mix together crumbs and butter then press into a pie pan. Bake at 375° for 7-10 minutes.

Luscious Lime Pie

My mom has been making this for years. This pie is especially for lime fans, who like things super limey!

1 cup plus 5 tablespoons white sugar
¼ cup flour
3 tablespoons cornstarch
¼ teaspoon salt
2 cups water
3 eggs
1 tablespoon butter, melted
½ cup lime juice
2 tablespoons lime zest (zest the limes before you juice them)
¼ teaspoon cream of tartar
9-inch pie crust, baked

Preheat oven to 425°. Separate the egg yolks from the whites. Beat the yolks and set the whites aside. Combine one cup white sugar, flour, cornstarch and salt in a saucepan. Stir in the water. Cook over medium heat until thickened. Gradually stir the cooked sugar mixture into the beaten egg yolks, beating constantly. Return the mixture to low heat and cook, stir constantly for two minutes. Stir in the butter, lime juice and lime zest. Set aside and let mixture cool slightly. Beat egg whites until light and frothy. Add cream of tartar and continue beating until stiff peaks form. *I find the whites increase faster if you use a cold bowl and cold beaters.* Gradually beat in 5 tablespoons of white sugar until the meringue is glossy. Pour the lime filling into pie shell. Pile high the meringue on top, spreading it until it touches the edges of the pastry shell. If you do not go all the way to the edges, the meringue will pull away as it bakes. Bake pie for 6 minutes or until meringue is golden brown. Let pie sit on the counter for an hour to cool before chilling in the refrigerator at least two hours before serving.

Three Ingredient Chocolate Mousse

This rich mousse is something I make more than any other dessert we have. It could not be easier and it is great for your fanciest dinner party.

1 cup semi sweet chocolate chips
5 tablespoons boiling water or hot coffee (regular, decaf or instant all work)
4 eggs, separated

Grind chocolate chips in a blender, using short pulses. Add boiling water and blend to melt the chocolate. Take a knife and check the corners of the blender as some of the chips get stuck there. Add yolks, one at a time, blending one minute after each. In a bowl, beat egg whites until stiff peaks form. Fold into chocolate gently. Chill in refrigerator at least two hours. This can also be made the night before you serve it.

Marcia's Coffee Crunch

My mother-in-law made this for her family as they grew up and we often have a pan of it in our freezer. It must be stored in the freezer as well. Make it a day ahead too.

1 box shortbread cookies, crushed (I like Lorna Doone)
½ cup butter, melted
2 cups powdered sugar
1 cup butter, softened
6 eggs, divided
4 teaspoons instant coffee crystals (decaf works great too)
2 squares sweetened chocolate, melted
1 teaspoon vanilla extract
6 toffee candy bars, chopped (I like Heath candy bars)

Mix cookies with ½ cup melted butter and press into 9x13-inch pan. Beat ½ cup butter and sugar until fluffy. Add 6 yolks, coffee crystals, chocolate and vanilla. In other bowl, beat 6 whites to stiff peaks; fold into coffee mixture. Top with candy bars, put in the freezer for several hours before serving!

Strawberry Pizza Pie

Our friend Jordan said this was the best strawberry dessert he had ever tasted.

2 cups flour
½ cup powdered sugar
1 ¼ cups white sugar, divided
1 cup butter, softened
8 ounce package cream cheese, softened
8 ounce container strawberry cream cheese, sortened
1 teaspoon vanilla extract
4 cups strawberries, sliced
2 cups strawberries, mashed (I use a potato masher)
2 tablespoons cornstarch

Preheat oven to 350°. Mix together flour, ½ cup powdered sugar and butter. Use your hands to bring the dough together then press it into a round pizza pan. Bake for 15 -18 minutes, then cool to room temperature. Beat both cream cheese, vanilla and ¾ white cup sugar together and spread over crust. Place sliced berries over the cream cheese filling. In a medium sauce pan, cook mashed berries, ½ cup white sugar and cornstarch until the sauce thickens a bit. Pour sauce into a mesh strainer and push the liquid thru with a spatula until all you have left are strawberry pieces. Pour sauce evenly over the arranged berries and chill for a few hours.

Brown Sugar Fruit Crisp

I made this recipe up in high school. Try some cream on top for a yummy breakfast.

4 cups fresh fruit; rhubarb, apples, peaches or berries (if frozen, it must first be thawed and you may need more than 4 cups)
½ cup butter, softened
1 cup flour
1 cup brown sugar, firmly packed
Big handful rolled oats (quick or old-fashioned)

Preheat oven to 350°. With your hands, crumble together butter, flour, brown sugar and rolled oats until it is a coarse meal. Place the fruit in shallow dish, cover with crumbled topping and bake for an hour. Great hot, room temperature or cold.

Mrs. Stinglehoof's Peach Cobbler

Warm, sweet and bursting with flavor. Served with vanilla ice cream, it can't be beat!

8 fresh peaches, sliced *or* 5 - 15.25 ounces cans of peaches, drained
¼ cup white sugar
¼ cup brown sugar, firmly packed
¼ teaspoon cinnamon
⅛ teaspoon nutmeg
1 teaspoon lemon juice
2 teaspoons cornstarch

Preheat oven to 425°. Combine peaches, both sugars, cinnamon, nutmeg, lemon juice and cornstarch. Toss to coat the peaches then pour into 9x13-inch. Bake for 10 minutes, then remove and set aside.

Topping:
2 cups flour
½ cup plus 3 tablespoons white sugar
½ cup brown sugar, firmly packed
2 teaspoons baking powder
½ teaspoon salt
1 cup cold unsalted butter, cut in small pieces
½ cup boiling water
1 teaspoon ground cinnamon

Combine flour, ½ cup white sugar, brown sugar, baking powder and salt. Add butter and process this with your hands until it resembles a coarse meal. Add water until it is just combined. Do not over mix it. Drop topping in blobs on the peaches, covering as much of the peaches as you can. Mix together three tablespoons white sugar and one teaspoon cinnamon. Sprinkle the cinnamon/sugar mixture evenly over the topping and bake for 30 minutes in a 425° oven.

Triple Berry Island

This looks beautiful and is very refreshing with the lemon, sweet whipped cream, fresh berries and crunchy pastry.

1 - 17.25 ounce package puff pastry sheets, thawed
¼ cup lemon juice
1 tablespoon lemon zest
1 - 14 ounce can sweetened condensed milk
2 cups sweetened whipped cream
1 pint strawberries, hulled and sliced
1 pint blueberries
1 pint raspberries
White sugar for garnish

Preheat oven to 400°. Roll each sheet of puff pastry into 10x13-inch rectangle on a lightly floured surface. Take one sheet of pastry and put it on a sheet pan that has been sprayed with cooking spray. Take the second sheet and using a pizza cutter, cut four strips that are 13 inches long by one inch wide. Reserve remaining dough for decoration. Brush edges of the large single sheet of pastry with water. Lay the four strips of pastry over all four edges making an outer rim. Trim off any excess dough. Prick entire bottom of large sheet with a fork and bake for 15 minutes. It may puff up but it will flatten as it cools. Cool completely. Using a cookie cutter, cut shapes from remaining dough; sprinkle each with sugar and bake for 12 minutes in a 400° oven. In a bowl, whisk lemon juice, condensed milk and zest. Fold in to that 1½ cups of whipped cream then spread it on your cooled pastry shell. Add all three types of berries evenly over that and top with pastry decorations. Place the remaining ½ cup of whipped cream in a few places on top of the berries for a decorative touch.

Food Fact:
There is more real lemon juice in lemon furniture polish than in most commercial lemonades.

Sticky Rice and Mango

I learned to make this from someone from Thailand. The special sticky rice can only be purchased at an Asian food store and it is the only kind of rice that works in this dish. It takes a bit of time to make this, but the end result is more than worth it!

2 cups sticky rice
2 cups coconut milk
¾ cup white sugar
Pinch of salt
3 mangoes, peeled and sliced (can also use pineapple, peaches, bananas or nectarines)
Toasted sesame seeds (optional)

Rinse rice until the water runs clear (it will take many times of rinsing until the water is clear). Place the rice in a bowl and add water three inches above the rice, then let it stand at least 5 hours. Drain rice into heavy cheesecloth and place your cheesecloth bundle inside a bamboo steamer that has a lid. Fill a deep soup pot half full of water and bring it to a boil. Place the steamer over the pot, place the lid on the steamer and let it cook for 45 minutes. While that is steaming, bring the coconut milk, sugar and salt to a boil, then take it off the heat and set aside. When the rice is done steaming, stir milk mixture into it and as it cools it will absorb all the liquid. Put the rice and fruit on your serving platter, pour the finishing sauce evenly over the top and sprinkle with sesame seeds, if using. I like this both room temperature and warm. My husband also likes it cold the next day for breakfast.

Finishing Sauce:
2 cups coconut milk
6 tablespoons white sugar

Stir together and set aside.

Orange Ricotta Tart

A great way to use extra ricotta cheese when making lasagna. This is refreshing and just as good cold the next day.

1 ¾ cups flour
1 cup white sugar
2 ½ tablespoons orange zest
½ teaspoon salt
½ teaspoon baking powder
½ cup cold butter, diced
4 large eggs
16 ounces ricotta cheese
4 ounces cream cheese, softened
1 tablespoon cornstarch
1 teaspoon vanilla extract

Preheat oven to 350°. In processor add flour, ½ cup white sugar, salt, one tablespoon of zest and baking powder. Add butter and blend until it is a coarse meal. Add two eggs and blend until clumps form. Turn onto floured surface and knead for one minute. Divide into two pieces with one slightly larger. Wrap the smaller one in plastic wrap and put it in the refrigerator. Press the larger piece over the bottom and up the sides of 9-inch tart pan. Beat ricotta, cream cheese, cornstarch and vanilla. Add the remaining sugar, 1½ tablespoons of zest and two eggs. Pour into prepared tart pan. Take other piece of dough out of the refrigerator and roll it to a 10-inch round. Place that on top of the tart; trim the excess and seal or pinch the edges together. Cut four slits in the top and bake it for 1 hour and 5 minutes. Cool before serving.

Food Fact:
Christopher Columbus brought the first orange seeds to the New World on his second voyage in 1493. Navel oranges have a belly-button bump opposite the stem end. The bigger the bump, the sweeter the orange.

INDEX

MAIN DISHES

MEATLESS MAIN DISHES